Praise for Kerry Dunnington's *This Book Cooks*

"We will see *This Book Cooks* on The New York Times bestseller list."

—Joe Pacino, WLG Radio, Baltimore, Maryland

"Kerry's creative flare, coupled with her years of professional experience in the kitchen, translates here into an exciting collection of marvelous recipes that are easy to follow and execute. Her approach melds tried and true culinary traditions with a fresh, modern approach, respecting the economic and time constraints of the modern kitchen, while stressing the importance of supporting our regional producers by shopping local and eating in season."

—John Shields, Chef, National PBS-TV Host, Author

"We have discovered a delightful cookbook that not only collects classics, but updates them with a twist."

—Al Spoler, Radio Kitchen WYPR, an NPR News Station

"Kerry Dunnington is committed to the mission of preserving food traditions and celebrating the harvest that Slow Food Baltimore supports. She is a regular contributor to our newsletter and website."

—Pat Sullivan, Co-President, Slow Food Baltimore

"*This Book Cooks* is not only a culinary success it is a welcome addition to any busy household. In the age of go, go, go, Kerry Dunnington has found a way to bring recipes that delight the taste buds and bring a welcome variety of healthy dishes to our tables. We were thrilled to welcome her to our shop for an author event and food tasting of her previous book, *Tasting The Seasons*. Kerry's books are a must have in the kitchen whether for a dinner party, a holiday or a tired Tuesday night, I love creating them and can't wait for Kerry's return to Moravian Book Shop!"

—Janelle Lockett, Moravian Book Shop

"I'm a working mother of two children who despite a very busy schedule is not willing to compromise on good nutrition. I am always looking for creative, tasty dishes that are not overly time consuming and yet will appeal to the diverse tastes of our family members. Your book is outstanding and practical. It offers many excellent, delicious and nutritious recipes that make cooking a joy. Not only am I complimented by my husband, a cardiologist who is concerned about consuming heart healthy foods, but the creative vegetable dishes that I have made using your recipes have also won rave reviews from my young children. Two of my favorite features of this book are that the recipes can be made in advance and that they are very visually appealing. Congratulations on an awesome cookbook!"

—Dr. Lisa L. Miller, Baltimore, Maryland

"*This Book Cooks,* has it just right. Like a musician improvising from a chord chart, Dunnington uses familiar concepts as springboards to create sparklingly flavorful and healthy dishes. Dunnington also gives families more than a dozen easy ways to combine healthy and delicious food with shopping choices and environmental consciousness. *This Book Cooks* encourages adventure without being daunting to a novice cook or a family exploring new tastes for the first time."

—**Cynthia Frank, cookbook collector, former caterer and restaurateur at The Well, a notorious six-night-a-week cabaret and coffeehouse in old Mendocino**

"Kerry's culinary influence and her superb cookbook, *This Book Cooks,* have turned us into cooks and the kind of hosts we never thought imaginable. If *This Book Cooks* represents all things Kerry, uncork the Veuve Clicquot La Grande Dame! In our opinion, Kerry yields: magnum opus."

—**Martha and David Frank, catering client**

"As a professional independent party helper, I've been working alongside Kerry for nearly 25 years, her passion and enthusiasm speak volumes in her work and her recipes, you can feel it when you're in her presence and you can feel it coming through the pages of the cookbook!"

—**Cindy Cook, Professional Event Assistant**

Praise for Kerry Dunnington's *Tasting the Seasons*

" … one of eighteen of the best books for food lovers."

—**Danielle Nierenberg, *Christian Science Monitor***

"*Tasting the Seasons* offers an innovative approach to seasonal cooking, with recipes to interest cooking aficionados and beginners alike. Commentary that informs and inspires a sustainable approach to home cuisine and entertaining accompanies the dozens of flavorful recipes Dunnington has included, creating an eco-friendly, all-occasion cookbook."

—***Mother Earth News***

"Dunnington has a unique way of profiling and combining unlikely ingredients that make her recipes appealing. With the greatest of ease, she folds in helpful tips, techniques and passion for what she is preparing."

—**Molly Kushner, Whole Foods Market**

"This is a practical cookbook. Each of the recipes in *Tasting the Seasons* has an introduction describing where it came from, any special ingredient and its contribution, and a short history of how it came to be. I felt as if the author was standing beside me; sharing a favorite memory, recipe and moment. I have made several recipes from this book; the preparations are not excessive or specialized. Lastly, the best review of this cookbook is that the recipes just taste delicious."

—**Ralph Peterson, San Diego Book Review**

THIS BOOK COOKS

ALSO BY KERRY DUNNINGTON

Tasting the Seasons
NATIONAL BENJAMIN FRANKLIN AWARD

THIS BOOK COOKS

Farm-Fresh Traditional Recipes
for Healthy Contemporary Cooking

KERRY DUNNINGTON

Artichoke Publishers
Baltimore, Maryland

Artichoke Publishers
220 Stoneyford Road
Baltimore, Maryland 21210
www.kerrydunnington.com

Cover photos by Whitney Wasson
Cover and interior design by Anita Jones, Another Jones Graphics
Illustrations by Elizabeth Stanley

ISBN: 978-0-9904185-1-1

Publisher's Cataloging-In-Publication Data
(Prepared by The Donohue Group, Inc.)

Dunnington, Kerry.
   This book cooks : farm-fresh traditional recipes for healthy contemporary cooking / Kerry Dunnington ; [illustrated by Elizabeth Stanley].

    pages : illustrations ; cm

   Illustrator information supplied by publisher.
   Includes bibliographical references and index.
   ISBN: 978-0-9904185-1-1

   1. Cookery (Natural foods) 2. Seasonal cooking. 3. Farm produce. 4. Nutrition. 5. Cookbooks. I. Stanley, Elizabeth, 1954- II. Title.

TX741 .D86 2015
641.3/02

Manufactured and printed in the United States of America

DEDICATION

I was a toddler when Julia Child was at the height of her career. Julia inspired women all over the country—including my mother—to *want* to cook, whether it was her complicated recipe for boeuf bourguignon or a simple version of meatloaf. She filled the hearts of would-be cooks with an all-important inspiration—that culinary endeavors were meant to be shared and enjoyed with appreciation and reverence. She left that legacy for millions of women who bought her cookbooks, watched her televised cooking show, and followed her recipes and instructions to create wonderful meals.

Cooking for a family of seven—and often for family, friends, and neighbors—in her Ruxton, Maryland, home, my mother honed her passion for great-tasting and nutritious food. The results were appreciated by everyone seated at our family table. My interest in cooking was inspired by many of the dishes she made throughout my childhood, the ones my brothers, sisters, and I requested many times over. The aromas wafting from our kitchen enticed us to take our places at the dining room table and enjoy her delicious, made-from-scratch creations. These are the memories I savor. This was the legacy my mother left to me.

The thought of turning her legacy into a book was an undertaking I never thought about doing until the urging of some friends whom I hosted for dinner. My mother thought this an excellent idea and encouraged me to turn my culinary creations—and so many of her creations that she shared—into a cookbook. The process from idea to final publication took several years—much longer than I expected.

When I published my first cookbook in 2004, I had absolutely no expectation of what the outcome would be. I was surprised and elated when the book became so popular. Through word of mouth and diligent self-marketing, soon I was selling hundreds of books. I was so passionate about the cookbook. Promoting it felt like an extension of my mother's passion for cooking and entertaining. I was having the time of my life!

Shortly after the book was published, I started writing another cookbook, *Tasting the Seasons,* and hoped after a few years it would be published. When I began working on that book, my mother was in the beginning of her eighth decade of life and in very good health.

I had every reason to believe that once it was published, she would be able to prepare the recipes, and, as always, the two of us would have long conversations about complementing menus and what to serve to whom whether it be a formal sit-down dinner, a teenage birthday party, a working meeting or a ladies luncheon. But *Tasting the Seasons* took much longer to finish and publish than anticipated. Her health declined, and she never saw the completed cookbook, nor did she see this book.

She would appreciate the enriched recipe introductions with the helpful time-saving tips and the attention to details to help readers more easily navigate each recipe. She once told me she never had time to read a cookbook from cover to cover and always accessed recipes through an index. The index is comprehensive, making it a quick reference for whatever food you're looking for.

Honoring my mother's spirit, I have infused this book with my own belief in the importance of implementing family food traditions and recognizing that our culinary choices have a major impact on the environment. I hope you and those you care and cook for, will embrace my conviction that we must shop the harvest, appreciate the bounty, and share in the goodness and nourishment that nature offers us.

Even as her health began to decline, I hoped to have *Tasting the Seasons* and a rough draft of this book published in time for her to at least enjoy reading the books. I knew she would take pride in my efforts. But in the end, as Parkinson's disease stole her ability to cook and read, all I could do was tell her about the cookbooks and my progress toward their completion. She died in 2013 just after her 90th birthday and before the books were released for publication. I owe my culinary career as a cookbook author and caterer to her, from whom I learned it all.

ACKNOWLEDGMENTS

Immense gratitude goes to Nick, my wonderful husband, and the official taste-tester of this cookbook. Thanks to family, catering clients, friends and neighbors and food and book enthusiasts for your love, support, and encouragement. Thanks to the following for your knowledge and support:

Kate Bandos

Sharon Castlen

Kate Gallagher

Anita Jones

Ann Lee King

Paul Krupin

Julie Murkette

Robin Reid

Elizabeth Stanley

Brad Walker

Whitney Wasson

The illustrator, Elizabeth Stanley, widow of Professor William (Bill) Stanley a world-renowned heart researcher, is a thirty-six-year veteran in education, currently living in Sydney, Australia. She has been creating art since her years in high school, achieving success as a wood carver. She is renewing her artistic endeavors since retirement from the school system.

CONTENTS

THE STORY OF "THIS BOOK COOKS"

My experiences in the kitchen began when I was about six years old. I prepared an imaginary meal for my brother in the kitchen of the playhouse our dad built for us. When my brother got tired of playing house, I could often be found standing on a stool beside my mother in our real kitchen helping her prepare our family meals.

The year I turned twelve, my mother relinquished the preparation of Sunday dinners to me. Since I'd been watching and lending her a hand for years, this privilege was a long-awaited opportunity. Not surprisingly, I fell in love with my new culinary responsibility and was complimented when my parents and siblings enjoyed the meals I prepared.

Fast-forward to my early twenties. Shortly after college, I accepted a position as an account executive for the Tremont hotels. My job was to book hotel rooms for movie stars who were performing in Baltimore. One of the properties I represented was an elegant and beautiful four-star boutique hotel that had a solid reputation for its high-end services. It was known as the ideal hotel for superstars. After a few years of securing rooms for celebrities (this was a complicated business: it involved demanding agents, an entourage, and a step-by-step guidebook for each celebrity), I was promoted to hotel general manager. For several years the wonderful employees who made up my dedicated team tended to the many, varied, and often unusual needs of the rich and famous.

An average day included working twelve to fifteen hours, typically six to seven days a week. The job absorbed me in every way, and even though at times it was very stressful, I loved the fast-paced, ever-evolving goings-on. No work day was ever identical. But on an idyllic spring morning, one of my jovial desk agents asked if I'd seen the fully bloomed cherry trees that lined the streets she knew were my route to the hotel. Confessing I hadn't noticed, I promised to have a look on my way home. The site of them took my breath away, and the experience stunned me into wondering what else I might be missing. After a few fitful nights of sleep and several days of contemplating my job and whatever else I was missing, I handed in my resignation.

Stay-at-home domestic bliss came quickly and easily for me after working twelve or more hours a day. Immediately I reunited with food and delved into a life centered on preparing meals for my husband, Nick, our family and friends. Days were filled with creating food combinations; each creation was sampled by Nick—the official taste-tester. If they got the ten-fingers flash, I penned a recipe. The recipes went into a recipe journal that grew rapidly over the next few months. I wanted to share my craft with a wider audience, and a few years after leaving the Tremont, I launched a catering business. Family, friends, and catering clients suggested that I expand my culinary career and turn my tried-and-true recipe journal into a cookbook. I did, and that was the beginning of my life as a cookbook author.

I'm grateful for missing the sight of those glorious cherry trees because that led to the beginning of my adventure in my culinary career. Over the years my recipes have happily filled the mouths of so many eager and willing tasters. There is nothing I find more pleasurable than designing food combinations, penning a recipe, lovingly preparing it, and gleefully sharing it with family, friends and catering clients.

THE 365 DAYS A YEAR ECOLOGICAL FOOD CHALLENGE

The idea of the ecological food challenge is to get your family to join you in making small, daily changes that will benefit the environment as well as their health. It's all too easy to get caught up in the hurried pace of everyday life and forget about how one item originated and all the processes it went through to land in our hands. By using the food challenge approach, we can make every day Earth Day if we focus more on recycling, reducing, and reusing—it's always better to reuse before you recycle—everything that comes into our daily arena. Some of these challenges are more mindful and creative, like the repurposing challenge. Others are educational, fun, and fulfilling.

THE SEED-TO-TABLE FOOD CHALLENGE

As gardening goes, is there anything more rewarding than planting seeds and watching them develop? Nurturing, harvesting, and consuming them? It couldn't be easier. Seeds, soil, and compostable egg cartons are the only tools you need to get this economical and worthwhile project started. The results are rewarding, visually pleasing, and healthy.

THE RAINBOW CHALLENGE

Is the food you eat in your daily round colorful—red, yellow, white, orange, purple, and green? Try incorporating as much color into your diet as possible. To do this, combine a variety of colorful fruits to your morning fruit bowl. To leafy green lettuce salads, add colorful vegetables like shredded purple cabbage, julienned carrots, yellow peppers, and Easter egg radishes. Using a combination of vegetables like carrots, green beans, cauliflower, mushrooms, and red peppers, create a medley-style side dish. When colorful fruits and vegetables are out of season where you live—for example, blueberries, blackberries, raspberries, strawberries, asparagus, and tomatoes— buy them traditionally preserved or frozen, or just opt out. Try and mix as much of the bounty as possible to get the full spectrum of colorful food.

THE RE-PURPOSING CHALLENGE

How much of what you buy do you repurpose? Set a goal and vow to repurpose one item each week. Here are some tips for achieving the goal of less trash in your household.
   1. Jars can be the holding vessel for a multitude of things; make them your everyday glasses and containers for your bulk pantry items. Standard jars that resemble Ball jars can

be used to traditionally preserve food. Make this challenge a family activity and involve your children. Try to come up with ideas about how to turn something into a useful item that you would otherwise throw away.

2. A handful of foods can be used to regrow more. Pineapple, fennel, sweet potatoes, ginger, lemongrass, romaine lettuce, garlic, celery, bok choy, cabbage, leeks, and scallions are foods you can regrow right in your garden. Look online for instructions.

3. Make your next table centerpiece using fruits and vegetables, and turn the centerpiece into cut fruit or a fruit-based dessert. Turn the vegetables into vegan entrees or vegetable side dishes.

4. Once you juice or consume citrus, turn the rind into candied peels. You can also cover the citrus peels with white vinegar to use as a scented household cleaner.

5. Instead of tossing those turnips and beet greens, add them to fruit smoothies.

WHO'S YOUR FARMER CHALLENGE

We get to know our teachers, politicians and neighbors, but what about our farmers? Do you know who is raising the food you are buying? What they are feeding the food you are consuming? Their methods for harvesting? Get to know the farmers whose food you're buying, whether they are in your community, in another state or region, or even on another continent. Look them up online to find out how they farm—you will be surprised by how much you can learn. Many farmers have a wonderful, multi-generation back-story, and others are just beginning their careers in farming.

THE SEASON-TO-SEASON CHALLENGE

Do your menus and meals follow the food seasons in your region? Eating local foods that are in season is good for you and for the planet. Food that travels long distances loses its nutritional content. Post a harvest chart for your area in your kitchen and follow the chart. Teach your children what's in season, and be steadfast with this mission. When nothing is in season, revert to traditionally preserved food, organic commercially preserved food, or frozen food. This is perfectly acceptable because food is preserved and frozen at the height of the season when it is at its highest nutritional content.

THE OLD-FASHIONED CHALLENGE

- Start traditionally preserving food. If this method isn't for you, purchase preserved foods from farmers you trust.
- Every time you cook a vegetable, save the vegetable water to make a healthy and great-tasting vegan broth. Freeze each batch until you have enough to make a pot of soup.
- For meat eaters, buy bone-in meat and whole chickens (it's less expensive and you're buying the cuts that aren't as popular—resulting in less stress on demand). Cook the bones, and use the broth as a foundation for soup.
- When and wherever possible, do business in trade.
- Go to you-pick farms. Make it a family outing.
- Whenever possible, purchase items packaged in glass, not plastic.

- Walk or bicycle.
- Support small, independent local businesses.
- Prepare food from scratch rather than from heavily processed ingredients (for example, make your own cookies from a favorite recipe rather than using the cookie dough found in the dairy case).
- Do not use a microwave oven—even if means pitching the one you have. Here are the two biggest reasons I don't use microwaves for cooking: 1) microwave cooking can reduce food's nutritional value; 2) I want to avoid the unsafe levels of electromagnetic radiation microwaves that can leak. Conventional cooking is not as fast, but its safety and nutritional value are more than worth the extra time.
- Bake your own bread. To my mind, this is one of the most rewarding culinary experiences. Is there anything more satisfying than a hot slice of bread or toast with your favorite spread—whether it's butter or almond butter, olive oil, or jam?
- Compost. It's simple and a wonderful way to give back to the earth naturally. Composting allows many of the foods we eat to come full circle. If you don't know how to begin, you can find good instructions online.
- If you find you are wasting food, change your shopping habits. Food is meant to be consumed, not thrown away. Learn to respect food and not tolerate waste. That's what our grandparents did. They found a way to turn what they had on hand into something nutritious and delicious. Be conscious of your buying habits. Be mindful of food that is about to turn. Before it does, freeze it, cook it, or add it to a recipe.
- Drink purified water.
- Sprout nuts and seeds. It's simple, economical, nutritious, and rewarding. A great project for kids. All you need is a sprouting jar and your choice of nut or seed.

THE PLASTIC DIET CHALLENGE

It's almost impossible not to buy *something* in plastic, but try to put the plastic intake in your cart on a diet once a month and then increase this to twice a month and so on. This is an exploration challenge. You will be surprised at how conscious you will become of how much is packaged in plastic.

THE AROMATIC FOOD CHALLENGE

The foods and spices we consume each have a distinct aroma. Some aromatic foods that come to mind are fresh-brewed coffee, fennel, peaches, cloves, and ginger. The scents of most herbs come to life when they are rubbed between our fingers. Many leafy greens and root vegetables have earthy or nondescript scents. A lot of the food we eat becomes very aromatic when cooked; for example, curry powder, meat, garlic, and onions. Is there anything more appetizing than the aroma of bread baking, apple pie oozing its cinnamon-laced apple scent from the oven, or the smell of a pot roast wafting from the kitchen? If the peach you pick up doesn't have an aroma, it's probably either not in season or not yet ripe. Be conscious of food aromas and what they do to your senses. Share food scents with your children, starting when they are very young. People relate food aromas to life experiences; this is part of what makes lifelong memories around food.

Eco Shopping Tips

REUSABLE GROCERY BAGS: While many grocery stores and even some states have banned the use of plastic bags, paper bags are still in wide use, and producing them gobbles up natural resources while causing significant pollution. Bags are made from tree pulp, so the impact on forests is enormous. If you don't already have them, buy reusable grocery bags. They are inexpensive, and they last for years. I throw mine in the laundry; they come out crumpled, but they are clean and still do the job. They're also more dependable than paper bags in wet weather. Store the bags in a location that is convenient and easy to remember so you will have them on hand when heading out for the farmer's market or grocery store.

REUSABLE PRODUCE BAGS: Reusable produce bags made of organic, washable cotton really reduce the use of plastic produce bags. In addition to using them for the fruits and vegetables you buy, they can be used as snack bags and for any bulk items.

SHOPPING THE PERIMETER: In supermarkets, and often even small grocery stores, the outer perimeter of the store's space is generally where fresh fish, produce, dairy, meat, chicken, and baked goods can be found. (An exception to this general rule is the ends of the aisles where high-margin goods are displayed to encourage impulse purchases—these are called crown-end displays.) It's inevitable that you will need certain items in various aisles, but be vigilant about what you're putting into your cart. Pay attention not only to product ingredients and their nutritional benefits, but also to the packaging and its environmental impact.

BUYING ONLY WHAT YOU NEED: Before you go to the market or grocery store, clean out your refrigerator and take inventory of your pantry items. This may sound daunting, but once you start doing this, you will avoid overbuying and ultimately save money. Also, this is the time to plan on turning the consumables you have on hand into a meal. For example, if you have any dairy that is inching toward its "use by" expiration date, you can plan to use it by making muffins, pancakes or waffles, a loaf of bread, or a milk-based soup or chowder. To make sure you will have all the ingredients needed, check the index of a cookbook for the best recipe and add those items not in your pantry or fridge to your shopping list. Think of this task as a mix and match game with food.

AVOIDING PLASTIC: We all know that glass is a better choice. (It's difficult to avoid plastic altogether, but wherever possible, choose glass.) I would be remiss if I didn't mention Styrofoam. Because it is not recyclable, I won't buy Styrofoam products or anything packaged in Styrofoam. On occasion, when I have needed an item in Styrofoam, I've asked for alternative packaging, and usually, store personnel have accommodated my request.

Eco Your Kitchen

COOKWARE: My favorite cookware is cast iron. Cast iron cookware conducts heat beautifully, goes from stovetop to oven easily, and it lasts for decades. For dependable and efficient cooking, nothing beats cast iron. I also recommend high-quality, 304-grade stainless steel and Le Creuset cookware. However, a drawback with Le Creuset is that, unlike cast iron, if you burn it, the cooking surface can't be restored. I don't recommend using any nonstick cookware because in many cases, it is known to emit toxic chemical emissions when overheated. Other cookbook authors offer different opinions on the safety of nonstick cookware, but I've not read or heard one that convinces me to switch from cast iron and stainless steel.

UTENSILS: Are you stirring your boiling soup with hard plastic utensils? They are typically made with Teflon, BPA, lead, aluminum, phthalates and/or melamine. These everyday kitchenware products have been tied to disturbing health issues. If you must use plastic, healthier alternatives are BPA-free, PVC-free plastic, #2, #4, and #5.

LEFTOVER CONTAINERS: There is so much plastic in our world, and too much of it ends up in landfills. So whenever I can, I buy glass. My mother and grandmothers had the most beautiful glass leftover containers—the good news is they are still available online. I buy the kind that have glass rather than plastic lids, and they do double-duty because they can be used for reheating. Use Mason jars, ceramic (with lead-free glaze that are not chipped or cracked), or high-grade stainless steel containers to store leftovers. If you must use plastic, refrain from microwaving food in plastic and do not place hot food in plastic—when you do, the plastic leaches BPA, an industrial chemical used to make certain plastics and associated with increased risk for certain health problems. Several types of plastic contain endocrine disruptors—substances that, when taken into our bodies, alter normal hormonal function.

PLASTIC WRAP: Here are some alternatives I use to avoid using plastic wrap to cover leftovers. Cover containers with plates that are a little bigger than the containers. You can also purchase washable dish covers made from organic cotton and linen fabric. Look for them online.

CLEANING PRODUCTS: If you're using baking soda, hydrogen peroxide, lemon juice, white vinegar, and Castile soap, you are making a healthy contribution to the health of your home and that of the planet. (My grandmother combined crushed, dried egg shells with baking soda. She used this mixture to clean the bathroom and kitchen sink, and her porcelain always sparkled!) If, however, you don't choose to use homemade cleaning products, look for cleaning products that have the DfE label, which was introduced by the Environmental Protection Agency (EPA) DfE means "design for the environment" and indicates that only the safest ingredients are used.

appetizers

INTRODUCING DIPS, SPREADS & IMPRESSERS

I love appetizers. That is why this is one of the largest chapters in this book. I could happily eat a variety of them as a meal instead of dinner. So I like to host and cater large cocktail parties because I can serve an array of appetizers (sharing my enthusiasm for them!) for several hours and keep people happy and fulfilled. This chapter is full of unusual, crowd-pleasing, and comfort-food appetizers. What better way to begin a festive evening.

There are lots of interesting (certainly not your run-of-the-mill) combinations in this chapter, and there is a lot of variety in the Dips and Spreads sections. In the Impressers section, you will find an array of vegan pâtés, fritters, and a variety of cheese combinations that always please. Cheese Curry Pâté with Plum Sauce, Apricots with Amaretto Cream and Teriyaki Walnuts, Cheddar and Pecan Pâté with Curried Caramelized Pineapple, Sun-Dried Tomato and Pesto Cheese Torte, and Apricot Meatballs are just a sampling of the mouth-watering recipes in this chapter.

DIPS

SPREADS

IMPRESSERS

GUACAMOLE

I'm a huge fan of avocadoes, and I love guacamole. There are two schools of thought about whether to store the avocado pit with the finished recipe in order to prevent the avocado from changing color. The adding-the-pit school of thought has always worked for me.

> *2 ripe avocadoes*
> *1½ tablespoons fresh lemon juice*
> *¼ cup minced onion*
> *1 medium tomato, chopped or ¼ cup salsa*
> *1 clove garlic, minced*
> *½ teaspoon salt (or more to taste)*

1. In a medium bowl, mash avocado. Add lemon juice, onion, tomato or salsa, garlic and salt, and mix until well blended.
2. Place the avocado pit in the mixture, and if you're not serving immediately, cover and refrigerate until serving time. Remove the pit just before serving.

Serves 6 to 8

REFRIED BEAN DIP

This is a zesty tasting, can't-stop-eating dip. Bite-size tortilla chips are perfect for dipping.

2 medium, ripe avocadoes
2 tablespoons freshly squeezed lime juice
1 can (16 ounces) refried beans
1 jar (12 ounces) hot salsa
1 cup sour cream
1 cup shredded Monterey Jack cheese
1 medium shallot, minced

1. In a large bowl, mash the avocadoes with a fork. Add lime juice, refried beans, salsa, sour cream, Monterey Jack cheese, and minced shallot. Combine until well blended.
2. Cover and refrigerate for 2 hours or more. Allow the bean dip to come to room temperature before serving.

Serves a crowd of 15 to 20

CREAM OF CRAB DIP

A plain, bland cracker is a good choice for this popular dip.

> *8 ounces light cream cheese, softened*
> *½ cup mayonnaise*
> *¼ cup minced fresh parsley*
> *¼ cup minced red pepper*
> *1 teaspoon Worcestershire sauce*
> *½ teaspoon salt*
> *1 pound lump crabmeat, picked of shell*

1. Preheat oven to 325°F.
2. In a large bowl, combine cream cheese, mayonnaise, parsley, red pepper, Worcestershire sauce, and salt. Fold crabmeat into cream cheese mixture.
3. Transfer mixture to a 2-quart baking dish. Bake for 45 minutes or until heated through. Serve immediately.

Serves 12

CREAMY SHRIMP DIP

For optimum flavor, prepare this dip a day in advance. Serve with a neutral-flavored cracker.

8 ounces light cream cheese, softened
1 tablespoon fresh lemon juice
⅓ cup chopped onion
2 tablespoons mayonnaise
1 teaspoon salt
A few grindings of freshly ground black pepper
1 teaspoon Worcestershire sauce
1 teaspoon sugar
1 pound cooked shrimp, peeled, deveined and chopped

1. In a large bowl, combine cream cheese, lemon juice, onion, mayonnaise, salt, pepper, Worcestershire sauce, and sugar. Mix until well blended. Fold in shrimp.
2. Transfer to a rimmed serving dish. Cover and chill overnight.

Serves 12

ZESTY ARTICHOKE DIP

It is believed that a version of this dip (see page 12 for The Classic Cheese and Artichoke Dip) was served at just about every party ever hosted in the 1950s and 1960s. It was commonly known as the "to-die-for, no-fail dip." With a mere four ingredients, it was simple to assemble, could be prepared in advance, and it was always devoured. Why would any hostess want to serve anything else? In my rendition (still simple), I've add creamy, zesty tasting Valbreso French feta cheese, garlic, and, for color, pimiento. The result has the same can't-stop-eating effect it did decades ago. Unless your guests detect the artichokes, this is almost always mistaken for crab dip. The flavors speak for themselves, so it's best to serve with a neutral-flavored cracker.

1 can (14 ounces) water-packed artichoke hearts, drained and chopped
1 cup crumbled feta cheese
½ cup freshly grated Parmesan cheese
1 cup mayonnaise
1 garlic clove, minced
¼ cup chopped pimiento

1. Preheat oven to 350°F.
2. In a medium bowl, combine artichokes, feta, Parmesan, mayonnaise, garlic, and pimiento.
3. Transfer to a 1-quart baking dish. Bake for 30-45 minutes or until light brown and bubbly. Serve immediately.

8 to 10 servings

EASY CREAMY BEAN DIP

If you're harried or really pressed for time, this is a quick and easy recipe, and it's nutritional to boot! Any white bean—cannellini, great northern, or navy beans—will work in this recipe. Serve with crostini, tortilla chips, or sturdy fresh vegetables.

2 cans (15 ounces each) white beans, drained
1 cup coarsely chopped red pepper
½ cup coarsely chopped onion
½ cup coarsely chopped parsley
¼ cup fresh lemon juice
2 cloves garlic
1 teaspoon salt
Several grindings of freshly ground black pepper

1. In a food processor combine beans, red pepper, onion, parsley, lemon juice, garlic, salt, and black pepper. Process until mixture is smooth and creamy.
2. Transfer to a bowl and serve immediately or cover and refrigerate until serving time.

10 to 15 servings

CREAMY MEDITERRANEAN DIP

This savory combination is always well-received. It's rather simple to assemble and best prepared in advance. Serve with raw vegetables or crisp crackers. I like to use Valbreso French feta cheese in this recipe because I love its robust flavor and creamy texture.

1 clove garlic
1 cup crumbled feta cheese
4 ounces light cream cheese, softened
3 tablespoons olive oil
¼ cup pitted Kalamata olives
3 tablespoons chopped scallions (green onions)
½ cup chopped walnuts

1. In a food processor, pulse garlic until minced. Add feta cheese, cream cheese, olive oil, and olives and pulse until mixture is nearly smooth. Add scallions and walnuts and pulse until mixture is well blended.
2. Transfer to a serving bowl, cover and refrigerate for about 2 hours or overnight. Allow the dip to come to room temperature before serving.

8 to 10 servings

SAVORY CHEESE
AND ONION DIP

I've been serving this savory, crowd-pleasing appetizer for decades. It's predictably devoured every time. If you're serving hearty eaters, I recommend doubling or tripling the recipe. A hearty rye or wheat cracker or crostini complements this three-ingredient wonder.

3 cups shredded Swiss cheese
1½ cups chopped onion
⅔ cup mayonnaise

1. Preheat oven to 350°F.
2. In a large bowl, combine the Swiss cheese with the onion and mayonnaise.
3. Transfer mixture to a 1-quart baking dish.
4. Bake for 15-20 minutes or until light brown and bubbly. Serve immediately.

8 to 10 servings

SMOKED FISH AND HORSERADISH DIP

Prepare this a day in advance, or the morning you serve it, to allow the flavors to mingle. Small leaves of Belgian endive or crispy crackers are flattering accompaniments.

⅓ cup prepared horseradish
¼ cup sour cream
¼ cup mayonnaise
⅓ cup thinly sliced scallions (green onions), green part only
1 medium tomato, seeded and finely diced
½ pound boneless smoked white fish (skin removed), crumbled into bite-sized pieces

1. In a large bowl, combine horseradish, sour cream, and mayonnaise. Add scallions, tomatoes, and fish, then mix until well blended.
2. Cover and refrigerate until serving time. Allow to come to room temperature before serving.

Serves 12

THE CLASSIC CHEESE AND ARTICHOKE DIP

This is a classic combination that I can't take credit for (although I use freshly grated Parmesan cheese instead of Parmesan cheese from a canister that, in my opinion, tastes nothing like fresh grated). But I couldn't resist adding this to the collection of appetizers, really as a tribute to the 1950s and 1960s when this was served at just about every party. It also evokes wonderful memories of all the parties my parents hosted. It's as popular now as it was then. Serve this dip with a crisp, neutral-flavored cracker.

1 can (14 ounces) water-packed artichoke hearts, drained and chopped
½ cup freshly grated Parmesan cheese
1 cup shredded mozzarella cheese
½ cup mayonnaise

1. Preheat oven to 350°F.
2. In a medium bowl, combine artichoke hearts, Parmesan cheese, mozzarella cheese, and mayonnaise.
3. Transfer the mixture to a 1-quart baking dish. Bake for 35-45 minutes or until the top is light brown and the cheese is bubbling. Serve immediately.

Serves 8 to 10

CREAMY CHIPPED BEEF AND CHEESE DIP

My mother prepared chipped beef dishes in many delicious ways; one of my favorites was this dip. It's an old-fashioned, revitalized recipe that I classify as comfort food. Accompany with a hearty cracker.

8 ounces cream cheese, softened
2 tablespoons milk
½ cup sour cream
¼ cup chopped onion
4 ounces chipped beef, chopped
A few grindings of freshly ground black pepper
½ cup chopped walnuts

1. Preheat oven to 350°F.
2. In a medium bowl, combine cream cheese, milk, sour cream, onion, chipped beef, and pepper.
3. Transfer mixture to a 1-quart baking dish and top with walnuts. Bake for 15 minutes or until mixture bubbles slightly. Serve immediately.

8 to 10 servings

CREAMY HOT PEPPER SPREAD

Every summer we buy several jars of homemade pepper jelly or jam from the local farmer's market. One warm summer evening I combined these ingredients, and the result was a delicious combination of sweet, sour, and hot with a creamy texture. Serve with a plain crisp cracker.

8 ounces light cream cheese, softened
1 cup shredded sharp white cheddar cheese
⅓ cup pepper jelly or jam

1. In a medium bowl, combine cream cheese, cheddar cheese, and pepper jam. Mix until well blended.
2. Serve immediately or cover and refrigerate until serving time. Allow mixture to come to room temperature before serving.

Serves 8 to 10

PISTACHIO GRUYERE CHEESE SPREAD

It may seem like an unlikely combination (and it is), but it's always well-received. Serve with crostini or a crispy cracker.

½ cup mayonnaise
½ teaspoon dry mustard
¼ teaspoon garlic powder
3 tablespoons white wine
½ cup minced fresh onion
2 cups shredded Gruyere or Swiss cheese
½ cup finely chopped pistachio nuts

1. In a large bowl, whisk mayonnaise with dry mustard and garlic powder. Add white wine and whisk until well blended. Add onion, cheese, and pistachio nuts. Stir until ingredients are evenly distributed.
2. Transfer to a rimmed serving dish and serve immediately, or cover and refrigerate until serving time. Allow to come to room temperature before serving.

Serves 10 to 12

WONTON CHIPS

The crispness of these chips is similar to the crispness of a potato chip, but the flavor is altogether different. I season these chips with Vege-Sal (look for it in the spice aisle of your favorite health-oriented grocery store), a wonderful flavored, all-purpose vegetable mineral salt seasoning. You can prepare any desired amount of wonton chips you like. One package yields about 48 wontons. (After you've cut them into triangles, you will wind up with 192 bite-sized chips.) These chips are perfectly satisfying on their own, but if you want to serve them with a dip, it's best to serve with a soft dip as they are really crispy and tend to break. If stored in an airtight container, wonton chips will last for several days.

> *Neutral cooking oil*
> *Wonton wrappers*
> *Vege-Sal seasoning*

1. To prepare a work surface for the cooked wonton chips, cover a portion of counter space with a brown paper bag (this absorbs the oil that drips from the wire rack), and place a wire rack over the paper.
2. Cut desired amount of wonton wrappers into four triangles.
3. Pour 3-4 inches of oil into large pot, and place over moderately high heat.
4. When oil is hot enough (to test the temperature of the oil, drop in 1 triangle; if it floats to the top immediately, the oil is ready), add the number of triangles that will fit the circumference of the pot. Keep the wonton triangles moving with a wide-mouth slotted spoon. When they begin to turn light brown, remove immediately and transfer to the wire rack. (As the oil gets hotter, wontons begin to cook rapidly; adjust cooking temperature accordingly and watch closely.)
5. Season the wonton chips immediately with Vege-Sal.
6. When wonton chips have cooled, transfer to an airtight container until serving time.

APRICOT MEATBALLS

People devour these meatballs. The meatballs and apricot sauce can be prepared in advance; combine the two, however, just before baking. I use Annie's Naturals brand French dressing in this recipe because I like the authentic, close-to-homemade taste. I'm partial to the French onion dip mix from Simply Organic.

MEATBALLS
2 eggs
1 teaspoon salt
Several grindings of freshly ground black pepper
1 cup herb-flavored dry bread crumbs
2 pounds ground chuck
1-2 tablespoons neutral oil

APRICOT SAUCE
8 ounces French dressing
1 cup apricot preserves
1 package French onion dip mix

1. Preheat oven to 350°F.
2. To prepare the meatballs, beat eggs in a large bowl until well combined. Add salt, black pepper, and bread crumbs, then stir until well blended. Add ground chuck to egg/bread crumb mixture and mix thoroughly. Shape the mixture into meatballs.
3. In a sauté pan, heat oil over moderate heat and cook meatballs until light brown and cooked through. Drain off fat. Transfer meatballs to a baking dish to accommodate.
4. To prepare the apricot sauce, combine French dressing, apricot preserves, and French onion dip mix in a medium bowl. Pour apricot mixture over meatballs and gently stir to combine.
5. Cover and bake for 30-40 minutes or until sauce is bubbling. Serve immediately.

30 to 35 meatballs

MARINATED SHRIMP

The call for a lot of salt and lemon juice is what gives this shrimp its outstanding flavor. So flavorful, takers are always clamoring for more, more, more!

5 pounds (16-20 count) shrimp
2 tablespoons salt
2 tablespoons dry mustard
½ cup neutral oil
2 tablespoons seasoned rice vinegar
1 cup fresh lemon juice (6-8 lemons)
2 cloves garlic, crushed
8-10 drops Tabasco sauce or hot pepper sauce

1. Fill a large pot with water and bring water to a boil. Add shrimp, reduce heat slightly, and cook for 3-5 minutes (stirring every 30 seconds or so) until shrimp are opaque and slightly firm. (Be careful not to overcook shrimp—they can get rubbery if they're cooked too long.) Drain shrimp and transfer to a bowl. Allow the shrimp to cool. Once the shrimp are cool enough to handle, peel and devein. Place prepared shrimp in a large container with a secure lid.
2. In a large bowl, combine the salt with the dry mustard. Add oil and whisk until salt and mustard are incorporated. Add vinegar, lemon juice, garlic, and Tabasco or hot pepper sauce, then whisk until well blended. Pour marinade over shrimp.
3. Cover and refrigerate for 4-6 hours. (Every hour or so, invert container to ensure the shrimp marinate evenly.)
4. Just before serving, drain the marinade from the shrimp. Transfer to a serving platter and serve immediately.

About 90 shrimp

MARINATED ROQUEFORT

I sampled this unusual appetizer years ago at one of those noisy, jam-packed parties a bachelor friend was hosting. In typical bachelor style, everyone was asked to bring food to share. After a few bites of this marinated cheese dish, I knew I wanted to find the guest who prepared this amazing taste combination. Once I found her, I could barely hear her say, *"Smother Roquefort with tons of thinly sliced red onion, and pour an oil and vinegar dressing over it and let it sit for a while."* I prepared it for the next party we were hosting, and it was a huge hit. The amount of red onion may seem excessive, but it withers and marries beautifully into the cheese. Serve with celery sticks, crispy crackers, or crostini. (Marinated Roquefort is also delicious used as a dressing for salad ingredients.)

½ pound Roquefort
1 medium red onion, cut in half and thinly sliced
¼ cup olive oil
1 tablespoon lemon juice
1 tablespoon red wine vinegar
2 cloves of garlic, minced
½ teaspoon dry mustard
½ teaspoon salt
½ teaspoon pepper

1. Crumble Roquefort into a 9-inch rimmed dish and cover with red onion slices.
2. In a medium bowl, whisk olive oil with lemon juice, vinegar, garlic, dry mustard, salt, and pepper. Pour evenly over Roquefort and red onion mixture.
3. Cover and refrigerate for several hours or overnight. Allow the mixture to come to room temperature before serving.

About 6 servings

Smoked Salmon Pâté

The addition of whipped cream cheese in this flavorful salmon recipe makes it lighter than most versions. Accompany with slices of pumpernickel bread, crostini, or unembellished crackers.

16 ounces light cream cheese, softened
8 ounces whipped cream cheese
2 tablespoons cooking sherry
2 teaspoons fresh lemon juice
1 tablespoon dried onion
2 teaspoons dried dill
½ teaspoon salt
A few grindings of freshly ground black pepper
4 ounces smoked salmon, chopped
Small capers and chopped red onion (garnish)

1. In a large bowl, combine cream cheese, whipped cream cheese, sherry, lemon juice, dried onion, dill, salt, and pepper. Fold in smoked salmon.
2. Transfer mixture to a serving platter and form into a round shape. Cover and refrigerate until serving time, or top with generous amounts of capers and chopped red onions and serve immediately.

Serves a crowd

Miracle Whip Shrimp

I feel obliged to include this recipe as a tribute to my grandparents because Miracle Whip debuted at the 1933 Chicago World's Fair that they so proudly attended. As a child, and until my grandparents passed away, I heard wonderful stories about the grandness of the World's Fair. When Miracle Whip was introduced at the fair, it promised to create, "Salad Miracles with Miracle Whip Salad Dressing." The whip was an instant hit!

My grandmother passed this popular recipe on to my mother. My mother loved it so much that it was always at the top of her list when choosing an appetizer to serve when entertaining. She claims it's the Miracle Whip that's responsible for its outstanding flavor, and I agree. For optimum flavor, make this a day in advance. Accompany with a sturdy whole wheat cracker.

¾ cup Miracle Whip
1 teaspoon Worcestershire sauce
1 clove garlic, minced
¼ teaspoon Tabasco sauce or hot pepper sauce
1 teaspoon grated lemon peel
1 pound cooked shrimp, peeled, deveined, and chopped
1 cup thinly sliced white onion

1. In a large bowl, combine Miracle Whip, Worcestershire sauce, garlic, Tabasco or hot pepper sauce, and lemon peel. Add shrimp and onion to dressing mixture, and toss to combine.
2. Transfer to a rimmed serving dish. Cover and refrigerate overnight.

Serves 8 to 10

BACON-WRAPPED BREADSTICKS

Bacon lovers, this one is for you! These are a great choice if you're hosting a brunch because they are filling and everyone is usually starving come brunch time. I have experimented with several types and brands of breadsticks and found the Stella D'oro brand works best. Make sure to choose boxes with breadsticks that aren't broken.

24 slices of bacon (about 1½ pounds)
2 boxes Stella D'oro original breadsticks

1. Preheat oven to 350°F.
2. In a spiral fashion, wrap 1 slice of bacon around each breadstick.
3. Line breadsticks 1 inch apart in a single layer on a parchment-lined baking sheet.
4. Bake for about 15 minutes. Turn breadsticks and bake for an additional 10 minutes or until bacon is cooked until just crispy.
5. Allow breadsticks to cool slightly before serving.

24 breadsticks

THE CLASSIC COCKTAIL CRACKER

These crispy, cracker-like crowd-pleasers have a wonderful flavor and texture. I like their informal ragged-edge appearance.

8 tablespoons (1 stick) butter, softened
1 cup shredded sharp white cheddar cheese
1 cup Rice Krispies cereal
¾ cup unbleached all-purpose flour
¼ cup wheat germ
A pinch of salt
A dash of Tabasco sauce or hot pepper sauce

1. Preheat oven to 350°F.
2. In a large bowl, cream butter, then add cheese and mix until well combined. Add Rice Krispies cereal, flour, wheat germ, salt, and Tabasco or hot pepper sauce and combine until thoroughly blended—dough may be a bit stiff. Knead for a few minutes until well-incorporated.
3. Pinch off bite-sized pieces and place on a parchment-lined baking sheet. With the back of a three-prong fork, make an indentation in the dough.
4. Bake for 15-18 minutes. Transfer the crackers to a wire rack and allow them to cool before serving.

Approximately 40 crackers (depending on size)

CHEDDAR AND CAULIFLOWER FRITTERS

More often than not, tasters don't detect the cauliflower and comment how much they love the *crab fritters with cheese!* I like the fritters' ragged appearance, so don't worry about forming them. Just pull off small amounts of batter and drop them into the hot oil. Fritter batter is best made a day in advance.

> *1½ cups unbleached all-purpose flour*
> *2 teaspoons baking powder*
> *½ teaspoon salt*
> *2 cups diced cauliflower*
> *1 cup shredded sharp cheddar cheese*
> *1 tablespoon minced onion*
> *1 egg*
> *1 cup milk*
> *Neutral oil for frying*

1. In a large bowl, combine the flour, baking powder, and salt. Add diced cauliflower, cheese, and onion. Stir until fully combined.
2. In a small bowl, whisk together the egg and milk, add to the flour mixture, and stir just to combine. Cover and refrigerate overnight.
3. In a large pot, heat 3-4 inches of oil over moderately high heat.
4. Drop small amounts of fritter batter into the oil (the fritters expand after they're dropped into the hot oil) and cook until golden brown. Using a slotted spoon, transfer fritters to a paper towel-lined platter.
5. Allow the fritters to cool slightly before transferring them to a serving platter. Serve immediately.

16 to 20 fritters (depending on desired size)

CHEESE CURRY PÂTÉ
WITH PLUM SAUCE

This is a mouth-watering combination that always receives excellent reviews, even from those who originally said they didn't like curry. For you curry fans out there, this dish is heaven. The flavors in this creation are bold, so it's best to serve with a neutral-flavored cracker. I use McCutcheon's Damson Plum Preserves in this recipe. It yields enough plum sauce for two to three cheese curry pâtés (depending on the sauce-to-pâté ratio you prefer) and will keep for several weeks in the refrigerator.

CHEESE CURRY PÂTÉ
8 ounces light cream cheese, softened
1 cup shredded sharp white cheddar cheese
2 tablespoons cooking sherry
1 teaspoon curry powder

PLUM SAUCE
1½ cups plum preserves
1 tablespoon apple cider vinegar
1 tablespoon packed brown sugar
1 teaspoon red pepper flakes
1 clove garlic, minced
½ teaspoon powdered ginger
Thinly sliced scallions (garnish)

1. To prepare the cheese curry pâté, combine cream cheese, shredded cheddar cheese, sherry, and curry powder in a medium bowl. Mix until thoroughly combined.
2. Transfer mixture to a platter and, using a spatula, form pâté into a round shape.
3. To prepare the plum sauce, combine plum preserves, apple cider vinegar, brown sugar, red pepper flakes, garlic, and powdered ginger in a medium saucepan. Stir until well blended. Bring mixture to a gentle boil. Remove from heat and allow the sauce to cool before storing. Keep at room temperature until ready to use.
4. Just before serving, spoon plum sauce over cheese and top with chives. Serve immediately.

10 to 15 servings

MARINATED BRIE
WITH PEACH PRESERVES

Serve this with a crispy, unembellished cracker.

1 round (6 inches) of Brie
2 tablespoons peach brandy
½ cup peach preserves

1. Place Brie in a 6-inch round baking dish. With a sharp knife, slice the top of the Brie as though you were drawing the lines for a game of Tic-Tac-Toe. Drizzle peach brandy into cheese incisions. Cover and refrigerate overnight.
2. Remove Brie from refrigerator 1-2 hours prior to baking.
3. Preheat oven to 350°F.
4. Spoon peach preserves over cheese and bake for 20-25 minutes. Allow the Brie to cool for 5-10 minutes before serving.

8 to 10 servings

SAGA CREAMY BRIE
AND PECAN WAFERS

This is great cocktail party fare. If you're not familiar with Saga Creamy Brie, it's a mild, blue-veined cheese with the flavors of blue cheese and Brie. It's delicious on its own, but it's also memorable in this wafer. If the yield is more than you need, you can successfully freeze half of the dough for another occasion.

8 tablespoons (1 stick) butter, softened
½ pound Saga Creamy Brie, softened
1 egg, separated (refrigerate and reserve egg white for use later)
1 cup unbleached all-purpose flour
1½ cups finely chopped pecans, toasted

1. In a medium bowl, cream butter and Brie until smooth and well blended. Stir in egg yolk and flour and mix until well combined. Add pecans.
2. Divide the dough in half and form into two logs (the logs should be the circumference of a 2-inch cracker); flatten each end. Cover and refrigerate overnight.
3. Preheat oven to 375°F.
4. In a small bowl, lightly beat egg white.
5. Slice logs into about ¼-inch slices and place on a parchment-lined cookie sheet.
6. Brush with lightly beaten egg white and bake for 10-12 minutes (check after 10 minutes), or until light brown.
7. Transfer to a wire rack to cool. Store in an airtight container until serving time.

50 to 60 wafers

CRISPY FRIED CREAMY VEGETABLE WONTONS

These tasty morsels are crispy on the outside and creamy on the inside—a combination of textures I adore. The flavor is further enhanced if you top them with a dollop of your favorite preserve or jam. Wonton wrappers are not perfect squares, so when you fold them corner to corner you will not get a perfect triangle.

4 ounces light cream cheese, softened
25 Wonton wrappers (about half of a package)
¼ cup thinly sliced scallions (green onions)
¼ cup shredded carrot
¼ cup shredded zucchini
A few dashes of salt
Neutral oil for frying
Preserves or jam for dipping wontons

1. In a medium bowl, combine cream cheese, scallions, carrot, zucchini, and salt.
2. Working with one wonton at a time, place about 1 teaspoon of the cream cheese mixture in the center of the wonton and fold over into a triangular shape. Dampen fingers with water and pinch seams together.
3. Set wontons on a plate, placing wax paper or plastic wrap between each layer to prevent the wontons from sticking. Continue filling each wonton wrapper until you have finished using the cream cheese mixture.
4. Heat oil in a large frying pan over medium high heat, and cook wontons (in batches) for 1-2 minutes on each side or until light brown. Serve immediately with preserves or jam.

Serves 10 to 12

Sun-Dried Tomato and Pesto Cheese Torte

This make-ahead party appetizer—pictured on the cover—is great to serve during the summer months when basil (the primary ingredient in pesto) is abundant. You can use your favorite pesto recipe or see page 145 for my recipe. The combination of flavors is pronounced, so it's best to serve this with crostini or a neutral-flavored cracker. I love to toss any leftover pesto with pasta.

8 ounces light cream cheese, softened
½ cup crumbled Roquefort cheese, at room temperature
½ to 1 cup pesto
¾ cup chopped sun-dried tomatoes

1. Line a 5- to 6-inch round container with plastic wrap; allow enough plastic wrap to hang over the sides.
2. In a medium bowl, combine cream cheese with Roquefort cheese and cream until well blended. Spread one third of the cheese mixture over the bottom of the lined container.
3. Top cheese with enough pesto to cover the cheese. Top pesto with ¼ cup sun-dried tomatoes.
4. Repeat, finishing with cheese. Cover and refrigerate overnight.
5. Invert torte onto a serving platter and allow it to come to room temperature.
6. Using the back of a spoon, make an indentation in the center of the torte. Just before serving, spoon the desired amount of pesto into the indentation and top the pesto with remaining sun-dried tomatoes. Serve immediately.

8 to 10 servings

CHEDDAR AND PECAN PÂTÉ
WITH STRAWBERRY PRESERVES

This recipe always receives high marks and with good reason; sweet and savory come together in perfect harmony. There's a significant yield, making it a great choice if you're hosting large gatherings or hungry appetites. Serve with a neutral-flavored cracker.

1 pound (5 cups) grated sharp white cheddar cheese
1 cup chopped pecans
1 cup minced onion
1 cup mayonnaise
A dash of cayenne pepper
A few grindings of freshly ground black pepper
1½ cups good-quality strawberry preserves
Snipped fresh chives (garnish)

1. In a large bowl, combine the cheddar cheese, pecans, onion, mayonnaise, cayenne, and black pepper. Mix until fully incorporated.
2. Transfer to a serving platter and form pâté into a round shape. Using a soup ladle, press the scoop part of the ladle into the center of the pâté making an indentation (this is where the strawberry preserves go).
3. Cover and refrigerate until serving time, or fill the center and top of the pâté with strawberry preserves and garnish with chives. Serve immediately.

Serves a crowd

Teriyaki Walnuts with Amaretto Cream and Apricots

These bite-sized morsels are a different twist from the typical appetizer fare. Invariably, takers always remark about their abundant pop-with-savory-sweet flavor. Choose dried apricots that give to the touch.

TERIYAKI WALNUTS
⅓ cup soy sauce or tamari
3 tablespoons dark rum
2 tablespoons toasted sesame oil
1 clove garlic, crushed
1 teaspoon ground ginger
4-6 drops Tabasco sauce or hot pepper sauce
1 tablespoon packed brown sugar
2 cups walnut halves
Salt (to season walnuts)

AMARETTO CREAM
8 ounces light cream cheese, softened
⅛ cup apricot jam
1 tablespoon almond amaretto liquor
1 pound dried apricot halves

1. Preheat oven to 350°F.
2. To prepare the walnuts, combine soy sauce or tamari, rum, sesame oil, garlic, ginger, Tabasco or pepper sauce, and brown sugar in a medium bowl. Add walnuts and toss with mixture. (The mixture is liquidy; it will thicken slightly and partially adhere to the walnuts as it cooks.) Transfer nuts to a parchment-lined, rimmed baking sheet. Bake for 15 minutes, tossing nuts halfway through cooking time. Using a slotted spoon, transfer walnuts to a lightly oiled piece of aluminum foil. Disperse nuts in a single layer and immediately season with salt.
3. To prepare the amaretto cream, combine cream cheese, apricot jam, and amaretto in a small bowl.
4. Just before serving, spoon about a teaspoon of the amaretto cream cheese mixture on to each apricot half and top with a teriyaki walnut. Serve immediately.

About 50 pieces

CHEDDAR AND PECAN PÂTÉ WITH CURRIED CARAMELIZED PINEAPPLE

Serve this crowd-pleasing appetizer with thin, crispy ginger snaps.

CHEDDAR AND PECAN PÂTÉ
8 ounces light cream cheese, softened
1 cup shredded sharp white cheddar cheese
¼ cup chopped pecans
2 tablespoons cooking sherry

CURRIED CARAMELIZED PINEAPPLE
1 tablespoon butter
1 teaspoon curry powder
1 cup finely chopped fresh ripe pineapple
¼ cup orange marmalade
Snipped fresh chives (garnish)

1. To prepare the pâté, combine cream cheese, shredded cheddar cheese, pecans, and sherry in a medium bowl. Mix until thoroughly combined.
2. Transfer mixture to a platter and, using a spatula, form pâté into a round shape. Using a soup ladle, press the scoop part of the ladle into the center of the pâté making an indentation (this is where the Curried Caramelized Pineapple goes). Cover pâté and refrigerate until about 1 hour prior to serving.
3. In a medium sauté pan over moderate heat, melt butter. Add curry powder and cook for about 1 minute. Add chopped pineapple, increase heat and cook until pineapple blackens slightly. Remove from heat. When pineapple has cooled slightly, add orange marmalade and stir until well combined. Keep at room temperature until serving time.
4. Just before serving, fill center and top of pâté with caramelized pineapple and top with chives. Serve immediately.

About 12 servings

soups & bisques

INTRODUCING SOUPS AND BISQUES

Nothing conjures up greater memories of my mother and grandmothers than when I prepare a pot of soup. They would collect the leftovers from our weekly meals and turn them into a delicious soup. We savored their creations, lapping each spoonful with relish. My mother elevated soup-making to what we referred to as classic high-quality French cooking. Like the French, she would cook the chicken carcass or beef bones in any leftover essence or water along with carrots, celery, onions, and sprigs of various herbs. After the mixture had simmered for hours and the essence was defatted, she added whatever leftovers she had on hand. No matter what the combination, she captured the flavors of the meats, vegetables, starches, and seasonings that went into each pot of soup she so lovingly prepared.

I loved coming home from school because the aroma that wafted from our cozy kitchen engulfed my senses. Something was always brewing from our Chambers stove, and I couldn't wait to get to the kitchen and discover what she prepared. There is nothing like soup to call to mind the love and thought that went into all those years of nourishment and instinctive thoughtfulness. So many of the soups in this chapter are representative of the creative combinations my mother put together. Nothing is more satisfying than to take the time to make a pot of soup. It fills the home with irresistible and inviting aromas and your partakers with lasting memories.

SOUPS

BISQUES

HALLOWEEN SOUP

My mother had a notion: if she fed her brood of five a hearty, stick-to-the-ribs irresistible dinner on Halloween, we wouldn't eat too much candy when we got home from trick-or-treating. This recipe defines stick-to-the-ribs and would be precisely the type of soup my mother would have chosen to serve on this kid-festive, candy-filled holiday. The combination of ingredients is most unusual, but don't let that deter you from preparing this delicious pot of soup. Strangely, peanut butter pulls the combination together in surprisingly perfect harmony. The combination of rice and beans makes this a complete protein, so it's hearty enough to be served as a main dish.

1 tablespoon neutral oil
1 medium sweet potato, peeled and cubed
1 cup chopped onion
1 cup diced red pepper
2 teaspoons cumin
½ teaspoon coriander
2 cups water
1 vegetable bouillon cube
½ cup minced fresh parsley
1 cup salsa (medium heat)
1 cup cooked wild rice
1 can (15 ounces) white beans
½ cup chunky natural peanut butter

1. In a large pot, heat oil over moderate heat and sauté sweet potato, onion, and red pepper for about 5 minutes. Add cumin and coriander, and sauté for about 1 minute. Add water, vegetable cube, and parsley. Cover and bring mixture to a boil, decrease heat to medium, and cook for 5-10 minutes or until sweet potato is tender. Add salsa, rice, beans, and peanut butter, and stir until peanut butter is evenly distributed. Serve immediately.

8 servings

ITALIAN WEDDING SOUP

I got this recipe from a charming young Italian couple who owned a quaint little café not far from where we live—the yield was for 100 servings! After several attempts, I managed to whittle it down to 4-6 servings and was happy when I got it to taste just like it tasted when I ate it at the café.

MEATBALLS
1 egg
⅛ cup dry bread crumbs
⅛ cup minced fresh parsley
1 teaspoon minced dried onion
¼ teaspoon garlic powder
½ teaspoon salt
Freshly ground black pepper, to taste
½ pound ground chuck

SOUP
3 cans (14.25 ounces each) chicken broth
1 cup julienned carrots
1 cup chopped celery
½ cup chopped onion
1 cup cooked white meat chicken cut into bite-size pieces
⅛ cup minced fresh parsley
½ teaspoon salt
Freshly ground black pepper, to taste
16 ounces frozen chopped spinach, defrosted, drained, and squeezed dry
2 eggs
3 tablespoons freshly grated Parmesan cheese

1. In a medium bowl, whisk the egg until well combined. Add bread crumbs, parsley, minced dried onion, garlic powder, salt, and pepper, and mix until incorporated. Add ground chuck and mix until thoroughly blended. Shape mixture into bite-size meatballs.
2. In a sauté pan over medium heat, cook meatballs until light brown and cooked through. Drain off fat and set meatballs aside.
3. In a large soup pot, bring chicken broth to a boil. Add carrots, celery, and onion. Decrease heat to medium, cover, and cook for about 5 minutes or until vegetables are fork-tender.
4. Add meatballs, chicken, parsley, salt, pepper, and spinach to vegetable/broth mixture.

5. In a medium bowl, whisk eggs until lightly beaten. Add Parmesan cheese.
6. Bring the soup back to a boil and add egg/Parmesan mixture. Do not stir. Cover immediately, and decrease heat to simmer and cook for 3 minutes.
7. Ladle soup into bowls, making certain each serving gets some of the egg/Parmesan mixture. Serve immediately.

4 to 6 servings

CREAM OF CARROT SOUP

This creamy soup has a wonderful velvety texture and a divine carrot flavor. It's a lovely soup to serve as a first course before dinner, or serve for lunch with finger sandwiches.

4 tablespoons butter
2 medium onions, sliced
4 cups chicken broth
4 cups sliced carrots
1 cup milk
1 teaspoon salt
A few grindings of freshly ground black pepper

1. In a large pot, melt butter over moderate heat and sauté onion for about 5 minutes. Add chicken broth and bring mixture to a boil. Add carrots, cover, decrease heat, and simmer for about 15 minutes or until carrots are fork-tender.
2. In a food processor or blender, purée soup in batches. Transfer puréed batches into a large bowl. In the last batch to be puréed, add milk, salt, and pepper. Transfer all puréed soup back into the original pot and stir until well blended.
3. Simmer soup until heated through. Serve immediately.

8 servings

BEEF AND BROCCOLI SOUP

This soup came together as the result of some leftover rice and broccoli and a few tomatoes that needed to be consumed. I often use Rapunzel Vegan Vegetable Bouillon Cubes (with sea salt) because I like the way it seasons food. The robust flavors from the cubes season this soup to perfection.

1 tablespoon neutral oil
1 medium onion, chopped
1½ pounds ground beef
5 cups water
2 vegetable bouillon cubes
2 cups cooked rice
2 medium tomatoes, chopped
1½ cups cooked broccoli pieces
1 medium carrot, shredded
A few grindings of freshly ground black pepper

1. In a medium skillet over moderate heat, heat oil and sauté onion until translucent. Add ground beef and cook until meat has cooked through.
2. In a large pot, bring water to a boil, add vegetable cubes, and stir until cubes have dissolved. Add cooked ground beef, rice, tomatoes, broccoli, and carrots. Bring to a second boil, cover, decrease heat and simmer for 10 minutes. Season with black pepper. Serve immediately.

8 servings

39

GINGERED COCONUT SWEET PEA SOUP

A simple and nourishing soup—pictured on the cover—that is delicious served with cornbread (see page 124) and a tossed salad.

1 cup milk
1 cup water
1 vegetable bouillon cube
1 pound peas
1 white onion, cut into chunks (about 1 cup)
1½ teaspoons salt
1 teaspoon ground ginger
A dash of cayenne pepper
½ cup raw slivered almonds
1 can (14 ounces) coconut milk
¼ cup fresh minced parsley

1. In a large pot, combine milk, water, and vegetable cube. Bring mixture to a boil over moderate heat. Add peas, onion, salt, ginger, cayenne pepper, and almonds. Cover, reduce heat to simmer (mixture should be rumbling), and cook for about 15 minutes or until the onions are tender.
2. Remove from heat and allow the mixture to cool slightly before transferring to a food processor or blender. Purée the pea mixture in batches until silky smooth. Add coconut milk and parsley to the last batch to be puréed. Transfer all puréed soup back into original large pot and stir until well combined. Serve immediately.

6 servings

CHICKEN AND DUMPLING SOUP

One of my fondest memories of visiting my grandparents was the aroma that wafted from their kitchen. Usually on weekends or holidays when we were visiting, my grandmother would make a chicken stock from a leftover chicken carcass. She would fill a large stockpot with water and seasonings and add chunks of onion, celery, carrots, parsley, and the carcass. The stock would simmer for most of the day. Sadly, most busy schedules don't allow us the time to prepare chicken stock. When time is of the essence, I use Imagine Foods Organic Free Range Chicken Broth. It's got that home-cooked, rich-tasting flavor, just like my grandmother's. This recipe is an adaptation from the soup my grandmother often prepared for our family.

CHICKEN SOUP
1 tablespoon neutral oil
1 medium onion, chopped
1 cup julienned carrots
1 cup sliced celery
¼ cup minced fresh parsley
1 pound skinless, boneless chicken breasts, cut into bite-sized pieces
4 cups chicken broth
1 teaspoon salt
A few grindings of fresh black pepper

DUMPLINGS
½ cup yellow corn flour
½ cup unbleached all-purpose flour
1 teaspoon baking powder
½ teaspoon salt
Several grindings of fresh black pepper
⅛ cup water
1 tablespoon neutral oil
1 egg

1. In a large pot, heat oil over moderate heat and sauté onion until translucent. Add carrots, celery, parsley, and chicken. Bring mixture to a boil. Cover and decrease heat to simmer and cook for about 15 minutes or until chicken is cooked through and vegetables are tender. Season with 1 teaspoon of salt and black pepper.
2. Fill a large pot with water and bring to a boil. When the water has boiled, decrease heat slightly; the water should be rumbling. Keep the water rumbling while you prepare the dumplings.

3. In a medium bowl, combine the corn flour, all-purpose flour, baking powder, salt, and pepper. Add water, oil, and egg, then whisk until mixture is fully combined. Shape mixture into balls, about 1 inch in diameter.

4. Add dumplings one at a time to the rumbling water. When all the dumplings have been added, cover and cook for 8-10 minutes. Using a slotted spoon, carefully remove the dumplings and transfer them to the chicken soup. Serve immediately.

4 to 6 servings

CURRIED BUTTERNUT SQUASH SOUP

Many years ago on a damp and chilly October evening, my cousin and his wife hosted a marvelous dinner party for family and friends. As a first course they served a delicious butternut squash soup. White bowls were brimming with sunset-colored soup, each garnished with slivers of emerald green chives offsetting the soup's beautiful color. The texture was silky-smooth, and it slipped down my throat like golden honey or a smooth single malt scotch. When the season for butternut squash rounds the corner, this soup (a rendition of my cousin's) is always on my list of must-haves. I use Imagine Foods Organic Free Range Chicken Broth because I like the rich authentic chicken broth flavor. For a perfectly delicious autumn dinner, I like to serve this soup as a first course, followed by the Sesame Pork Tenderloin with Mustard Cream and the Carrot and Leek Gratin (see Index for recipes), and a steamed green vegetable like green beans or Swiss chard.

4 tablespoons butter
3 leeks, white part only, thinly sliced
2 large onions, diced
2 teaspoons curry powder
8½ cups chicken broth
4 large Idaho baking potatoes, peeled and cubed
2 medium butternut squash, peeled, seeded, and diced
2 teaspoons salt
A few grindings of fresh black pepper
Snipped fresh chives (garnish)

1. In a large pot, melt butter over medium heat and sauté leeks and onion until glossy. Add curry powder and sauté until fragrant, about 1 minute. Add chicken broth, potatoes, butternut squash, salt and pepper. Bring mixture to a boil, cover, decrease heat, and simmer for 1 hour or until vegetables are fork-tender.
2. In a food processor or blender, purée soup in batches. Transfer puréed batches into a large bowl. After final batch is puréed, transfer soup back into the original large pot and simmer until heated through. Ladle soup into bowls and garnish with snipped fresh chives. Serve immediately.

14 servings

CREAMY CHEDDAR AND POTATO SOUP WITH BACON

This is a great soup to serve on a cold winter day with slices of dark, hearty bread and a leafy green salad.

2 large potatoes, diced
½ cup chopped celery
½ cup chopped carrots
½ cup chopped onion
About 3 cups water
1 teaspoon salt
4 cups chicken broth
½ cup milk
A few grindings of fresh black pepper
½ pound shredded white sharp cheddar cheese
6 slices crispy, cooked bacon, crumbled

1. Place potatoes, celery, carrots, and onions in a large pot with just enough water to cover the medley. Add salt. Bring mixture to a boil, cover, decrease heat slightly, and cook for about 15 minutes or until potatoes and vegetables are fork-tender. Add chicken broth.
2. In a food processor or blender, purée soup in batches. Transfer puréed batches into a large bowl. Add milk to the last batch and season with pepper. Transfer all puréed soup back into original large pot and stir to blend.
3. Heat soup over moderate heat and slowly stir in cheese. When cheese has melted, ladle soup into 6 serving bowls and top each bowl with crumbled bacon.

6 servings

Chicken and Leek Soup
with Wild Rice and Prunes

A neighbor gave me this recipe because she thought I would relish the call for prunes. She thought it odd, I thought it intriguing. The prunes give it a gorgeous chestnut color and a subtle, sweet flavor that pairs beautifully with the chicken and rice. This soup is one of our favorites.

> *1 cup thinly sliced leeks*
> *1 tablespoon neutral oil*
> *4 cups chicken broth*
> *½ cup (about 12) coarsely chopped pitted prunes*
> *2 cups cooked chicken breasts, torn into bite-sized pieces*
> *¼ cup chopped fresh parsley*
> *1 tablespoon toasted sesame oil*
> *1 tablespoon tamari or soy sauce*
> *A few grindings of fresh black pepper*
> *1 cup cooked wild rice*

1. In a large pot over moderate heat, sauté leeks in oil until lightly browned. Add chicken broth. Bring mixture to a boil and decrease heat to simmer. Add prunes, chicken, parsley, sesame oil, tamari, pepper, and wild rice. Cook until heated through. Serve immediately.

4 servings

CUCUMBER BISQUE

Many years ago on a sweltering summer night, my mother served bowls of cold cucumber soup from vessels she had placed in the freezer earlier in the day. The velvety consistency was so refreshing; spoonfuls slipped down my throat like a sweet, cold, creamy milk shake. So satisfying was this palest of green soup that serving it has become a summer tradition. When cucumbers are in season, this recipe takes center stage whenever my husband and I entertain. Complementary accompaniments are deviled eggs, slices of summer tomatoes, and my recipe for Moist and Rich Chili Cornbread (see page 126). This soup must be prepared a day in advance. Did you know summer's coolest vegetable is a fruit?

1 tablespoon butter
1 cup chopped onion
2 teaspoons unbleached all-purpose flour
2 medium cucumbers, peeled and sliced (about 3 cups)
1 cup chicken broth
1 cup plain yogurt
1 tablespoon chopped fresh parsley
½ teaspoon salt
A few grindings of fresh black pepper

1. In a medium pot over moderate heat, melt butter and sauté onion until transparent. Whisk in flour and slowly add chicken broth. Continue whisking until mixture is well combined. Add cucumbers to broth mixture. Cover pot and bring mixture to a boil, decrease heat, and simmer for 45 minutes or until cucumbers are fork-tender. Remove from heat and allow mixture to cool completely.
2. In a food processor, puree the cucumber mixture until smooth. Add the yogurt, parsley, salt, and pepper, and puree until velvety smooth.
3. Refrigerate overnight. Serve cold.

6 servings

VEGETABLE BISQUE

I love the versatility of this soup. Just about any vegetable will work. If you don't have some of the vegetables called for in this recipe, be creative and design a mixture of your favorite vegetables to use.

6 tablespoons butter
1 medium onion, sliced
1 leek, sliced (white part only)
4 cups chicken broth
½ cup white wine
¼ cup cooking sherry
1 cup tomato sauce
1 cup sliced carrots
1 cup peeled and diced potatoes
1 cup cauliflower florets, cut into bite-sized pieces
1 cup sliced celery
1 cup unpeeled sliced zucchini
1 medium sweet potato, peeled and cubed
1 teaspoon salt
Several grindings of fresh black pepper

1. In a large pot over moderate heat, melt butter. Add onions and leeks, then sauté until onions are transparent. Add chicken broth, white wine, and sherry. Bring mixture to a boil. Add tomato sauce and stir until combined. Add carrots, potatoes, cauliflower, celery, zucchini, sweet potatoes, salt, and pepper. Cover, decrease heat, and simmer for about 15 minutes or until potatoes and vegetables are fork-tender.
2. In a food processor or blender, purée soup in batches. Transfer puréed batches into a large bowl. After the final batch is puréed, transfer soup back into the original large pot. Simmer until serving time. Serve hot.

10 servings

entrées

INTRODUCING SEAFOOD, VEGETARIAN, BEEF, CHICKEN, AND PORK

If you're entertaining and want to impress with a seafood entrée, the Seafood Lasagna with Fire-Roasted Tomatoes and the Seafood Casserole and Creamy Seafood are wonderful. All of them can be prepared in advance—an element I appreciate because the entrée can get crossed off my "to do" list.

For vegetarians, there is a vast array of recipes. The Spicy Spinach and Polenta Lasagna, the Savory Cheddar Cheese Casserole, and the Spinach, Rice and Feta Casserole, are enjoyed as much by adults as they are by children. More exotic palates will relish the flavors found in the Spicy Mediterranean Couscous with Beans and Vegetables, and the Vegetarian Black Bean Enchiladas. Fusilli with Sun-Dried Tomatoes, Pine Nuts, and Feta offers a delightful combination of flavors and textures, and the Spinach and Mushroom Loaf is an unusual vegetarian take on the classic meatloaf.

In the beef section of this chapter there is an assortment of classic and elegant recipes, like my recipe for Filet of Beef with Bacon, Blue Cheese, and Sun-Dried Tomato Stuffing—Nick's all-time favorite. There are some comfort food dishes that are appreciated when the weather turns cool, including Beef Pot Roast, Tamale Pie, Simple Chili, and Braised Beef Brisket.

Three crowd-pleasing recipes for chicken are Ginger Glazed Chicken, Creamy Chicken and Zucchini Casserole with Herb Stuffing (comfort food even kids love—second helpings please!), and the elegant Spinach-Stuffed Chicken Breasts. Worthy of any holiday celebration or important dinner.

I often serve my mother's famous recipe for Baked Ham during special holidays like Christmas and Easter. The Soba Noodle Salad with Pears and Pork is fun to serve when you're feeling festive and daring to serve something unusual. Again and again, catering clients request the Sesame Pork Tenderloin with Mustard Cream.

So whether you're entertaining or just want flavorful everyday entrees, hopefully you will find recipes here that convince you to celebrate and share a culinary adventure.

SEAFOOD ENTRÉES

Creamy Seafood 51

Seafood Casserole 52

Spicy Shrimp over Lemon Parsley Rice 53

Seafood Lasagna with Fire-Roasted Tomatoes 54

Spaghetti with Shrimp and Artichokes in Spicy Tomato Sauce 56

VEGETARIAN ENTRÉES

Spinach, Rice, and Feta Casserole 57

Vegetarian Black Bean Enchiladas 58

Savory Cheddar Cheese Casserole 59

Spicy Mediterranean Couscous with Beans and Vegetables 60

Polenta with Roasted Peppers, Tomatoes, and Creamy Fontina 62

Fusilli with Sun-Dried Tomatoes, Pine Nuts, and Feta 63

Spicy Spinach and Polenta Lasagna 64

Spinach and Mushroom Loaf 65

Summertime Tomato Pie 66

BEEF ENTRÉES

Tamale Pie 67

Braised Beef Brisket 68

Marinated Beef Tenderloin 69

Filet of Beef with Bacon, Blue Cheese, and Sun-Dried Tomato Stuffing 71

Broiled Oriental Flank Steak 72

Chili Rellenos Casserole 73

Beef Pot Roast 74

Simple Chili 75

CHICKEN ENTREES

Ginger-Glazed Chicken 76

Creamy Chicken and Zucchini Casserole with Herb Stuffing 77

Spinach-Stuffed Chicken Breasts 78

PORK ENTRÉES

Soba Noodle Salad with Pears and Pork 79

Sesame Pork Tenderloin with Mustard Cream 80

Baked Ham 81

CREAMY SEAFOOD

This elegant dish is great spooned over rice or over slices of toasted bread. Complement with either of the aspic recipes or the Orange Marmalade Tomatoes (see Index for recipes) and steamed green beans. Just about any seafood mixture works in this recipe. I've had success using any combination of lobster, shrimp, and crabmeat. I use Imagine Organic Free Range Chicken Broth and Rapunzel Vegan Vegetable Bouillon Cubes with sea salt because they have such pronounced, authentic flavors.

> *2 cups chicken broth*
> *1 cup white wine*
> *1 cup water*
> *1 vegetable bouillon cube*
> *½ cup (1 stick) butter*
> *1½ cups finely chopped onion*
> *⅔ cup unbleached all-purpose flour*
> *1 cup heavy cream*
> *¼ cup cooking sherry*
> *1 teaspoon salt*
> *Several grindings of black pepper*
> *7 cups cooked seafood*

1. In a medium pan, combine chicken broth, white wine, water, and vegetable bouillon cube. Bring mixture to a boil. Decrease heat and stir mixture until cube dissolves.
2. In a large pan over moderate heat, melt butter and sauté onion until translucent. Whisk in flour a third of a cup at a time and whisk until mixture comes together. Slowly add hot chicken broth combination, whisking constantly. Whisk until mixture is smooth and well blended. Decrease heat to simmer. Add cream, sherry, salt, pepper, and seafood to broth mixture and stir to fully incorporate.
3. Simmer over low heat until hot. Serve immediately.

8 to 10 servings

SEAFOOD CASSEROLE

I often serve this elegant dish when Nick and I entertain because it always receives such high ratings. It's also a mainstay with catering clients. Colorful and complementary accompaniments are Brandied Carrots with Peas and Orange Marmalade Tomatoes (see Index for recipes).

1 pound jumbo lump crabmeat, picked of any shells
1 pound large cooked shrimp, peeled and deveined, cut into bite-sized pieces
½ cup finely chopped onion
½ cup finely chopped celery
½ cup finely chopped green or red pepper
1 cup mayonnaise
½ teaspoon salt
1 teaspoon Worcestershire sauce
⅛ teaspoon cracked black pepper
2 tablespoons butter, melted
1 cup good-quality white bread (French or Italian works well) cut into small cubes

1. Preheat oven to 350°F.
2. In a large bowl, toss crabmeat with shrimp.
3. In a large bowl, combine onion, celery, green pepper, mayonnaise, salt, Worcestershire sauce, and black pepper. Fold crab/shrimp mixture into mayonnaise mixture and gently mix until well combined. Transfer seafood mixture to a 2-liter baking dish.
4. In a small pan over moderate heat, melt butter, add bread cubes, and toss to combine. Top seafood salad with buttered bread cubes.
5. Bake for 25-30 minutes until heated through or bread cubes are light brown. Serve immediately.

6 servings

SPICY SHRIMP
OVER LEMON PARSLEY RICE

I use basmati rice in this dish because I like the way the cooked grains don't clump together. I also love to use this rice because of its fragrance—known as the queen of fragrance—with its savory, nut-like flavor and aroma.

2 cups raw white basmati rice
3½ cups water
2 teaspoons salt
2 tablespoons fresh minced parsley
2 teaspoons finely grated lemon peel
Several grindings of fresh black pepper
8 tablespoons butter
4 cloves garlic, minced
1 lemon, thinly sliced
1 teaspoon oregano
1 bay leaf
½-1 teaspoon red pepper flakes, according to your preference for spicy
1 teaspoon salt
2 pounds large raw shrimp, peeled and deveined

1. In a large saucepan, combine rice, water, and salt. Bring mixture to a boil, cover, decrease heat, and simmer for 15 minutes or according to package directions.
2. When the rice has finished cooking, immediately add the parsley, lemon peel, and pepper. Stir until well combined. Cover and keep warm.
3. In a sauté pan over moderate heat, melt butter and sauté garlic for 1-2 minutes. Add lemon slices, oregano, bay leaf, red pepper flakes, salt, and shrimp. Increase heat slightly and sauté shrimp for 3-5 minutes until cooked through. Discard bay leaf.
4. Divide rice among 6 rimmed serving bowls and top each bowl with the shrimp mixture. Serve immediately.

6 servings

Seafood Lasagna with Fire-Roasted Tomatoes

This is a sophisticated pasta dish—perfect if you're hosting an important dinner. To round out the meal, serve with Brandied Carrots with Peas and Moist and Rich Chili Cornbread (see Index for recipes).

SEAFOOD LASAGNA SAUCE
3 tablespoons butter
1 cup finely chopped onion
1 vegetable bouillon cube
2 tablespoons unbleached all-purpose flour
2 cups milk
1 cup chopped cooked shrimp
2 tablespoons cooking sherry
½ teaspoon salt
Several grindings of fresh black pepper
1 pound lump crabmeat, shells removed

LASAGNA
1 egg
2 cups cottage cheese
8 ounces light cream cheese, softened
1 cup finely chopped onion
¼ cup minced fresh parsley
1 teaspoons salt
¼ teaspoon pepper
9 no-boil (or oven-ready) lasagna noodles
1 can (14.5 ounces) fire-roasted crushed tomatoes
¼ cup minced fresh parsley
1½ cups shredded white cheddar cheese

1. To make the seafood sauce, melt butter in a large skillet over medium heat and sauté onion until translucent. Add vegetable bouillon cube and stir until the cube has dissolved. Whisk in flour, 1 tablespoon at a time. Slowly add milk, whisking constantly until smooth and well blended. Simmer for 10-15 minutes or until slightly thickened. Add shrimp, sherry, salt, black pepper, and crabmeat to milk mixture and stir until well combined. Set aside.
2. Preheat oven to 350°F.

3. To assemble the lasagna, whisk egg in a large bowl until blended. Add cottage cheese, cream cheese, onion, parsley, salt, and pepper.

4. Spoon one third of the seafood sauce (about 1½ cups) in the bottom of a 13 x 9-inch baking dish. In a single layer, top the sauce with 3 lasagna noodles. Cover the noodles with one third of the cottage cheese mixture—about a heaping cup. Top the cottage cheese mixture with one third of the seafood sauce. Lay 3 noodles over sauce and top the noodles with remaining seafood sauce.

5. Top seafood sauce with remaining 3 noodles. Top noodles with remaining cottage cheese mixture.

6. Evenly distribute tomatoes over lasagna and top the tomatoes with shredded cheese.

7. Cover and bake for 1 hour. Remove cover and bake an additional 15 minutes. Let lasagna rest for about 15 minutes before serving.

8 servings

SPAGHETTI WITH SHRIMP AND ARTICHOKES IN SPICY TOMATO SAUCE

This is an impressive, quick any-night-of-the-week meal. If spicy red sauce is more spice than you desire, it can easily be replaced with any of the number of tomato sauces that line grocery store shelves. I use Valbreso French feta cheese in this recipe because I like its creamy texture and tangy flavor. Serve this dish with slices of good-quality bread and a tossed lettuce leaf salad. For a nearly perfect portion of spaghetti, fill a 1-inch diameter empty spice jar with dry spaghetti.

> ¼ cup olive oil
> 4 cloves garlic, minced
> 1 red pepper, chopped
> 2 pounds raw shrimp, peeled and deveined
> 1 jar (26 ounces) spicy red tomato sauce
> 1 can (15 ounces) water-packed artichoke hearts, drained, and quartered
> Spaghetti (1 pound or portioned amount)
> 1 cup crumbled feta

1. Fill a large pot with water and bring to a boil.
2. While you're waiting for the water to come to a boil, in a large skillet, heat olive oil over medium heat and sauté garlic and red pepper for 3-5 minutes. Add shrimp and cook until shrimp are opaque. Add sauce and artichoke hearts. Reduce heat and simmer.
3. While the sauce is simmering, cook spaghetti according to package directions. Drain spaghetti and divide it among 6 rimmed serving bowls. Evenly distribute sauce over the spaghetti. Top each with feta cheese or pass to your guests. Serve immediately.

6 servings

SPINACH, RICE, AND FETA CASSEROLE

This is a great weeknight entrée. It's a dinner kids love and one they have touted as comfort food. Valbreso French feta cheese has a creamy texture and is just tangy enough in this flavorful casserole.

> *1 tablespoon neutral oil*
> *1 cup chopped onion*
> *2 eggs*
> *1¼ cups milk*
> *¼ cup sour cream*
> *½ teaspoon salt*
> *¼ teaspoon pepper*
> *3 cups cooked Basmati rice*
> *16 ounces frozen chopped spinach, defrosted, drained, and squeezed dry*
> *1 cup crumbled feta cheese*
> *3 tablespoons freshly grated Parmesan cheese*

1. Preheat oven to 400°F.
2. In a medium pan, heat oil over moderate heat and sauté onion until soft.
3. In a large bowl, whisk eggs until well blended. Add sautéed onions, milk, sour cream, salt, and pepper. Whisk until the sour cream is incorporated with the milk. Add rice, spinach, and feta to the sour cream mixture.
4. Transfer the mixture to a 2-quart baking dish that has been coated with cooking oil. Top with Parmesan cheese.
5. Bake for 35-45 minutes or until light brown and bubbly. Serve immediately.

6 servings

VEGETARIAN BLACK BEAN ENCHILADAS

I love to serve this hearty dish with the Hearts of Palm, Mango, and Cashew Salad with Salty Lime Dressing (see page 115).

1 tablespoon neutral oil
1 cup chopped onion
1 garlic clove, minced
2 teaspoons chili powder
2 teaspoons cumin powder
¼ teaspoon oregano
¼ teaspoon salt
⅛ teaspoon red pepper flakes
1 can (14.5 ounces) diced tomatoes
2 cans (15 ounces each) black beans, drained and reserved
1 can (4 ounces) chopped green chilies
2 cups shredded Monterey Jack cheese
6 (7-inch) soft flour tortillas
Snipped fresh chives (garnish)
Sides of sour cream and guacamole (see page 3)

1. Preheat oven to 350°F.
2. Heat oil in a large skillet over medium heat, then sauté onion and garlic until tender. Add chili powder, cumin, oregano, salt, and red pepper, and sauté for one minute. Stir in tomatoes. Set mixture aside.
3. Transfer 1 cup of the tomato mixture to a medium bowl.
4. Add drained black beans and green chilies to the tomato mixture in the sauté pan.
5. Lightly oil a 13 x 9-inch baking dish.
6. Working from a rimmed vessel or from the baking dish (to prevent the bean mixture from spilling over the work surface), sprinkle about ¼ cup of the cheese down the center of one tortilla shell and top with about ½ cup of the black bean mixture from the sauté pan.
7. Roll tortilla shell and place in the baking dish seam side down.
8. Repeat with remaining tortilla shells.
9. Spoon reserved tomato mixture over enchiladas. Top the enchiladas with the remaining cheese.
10. Bake uncovered for 45 minutes or until bubbly.
11. Divide enchiladas between 6 serving plates. Garnish plates with chives. Pass the sour cream and guacamole to your guests. Serve immediately.

6 servings

SAVORY CHEDDAR CHEESE CASSEROLE

The first time I served this was at a luncheon I hosted for a very special neighbor who was moving out of town. I accompanied it with Orange Marmalade Tomatoes and Broccoli, Sweet Onion, and Cashew Salad (see Index for recipes), and everyone appreciated the combination of flavors and the colorful plates.

Butter, softened
4 cups good-quality, day-old Italian or French bread (with crusts)
2 cups grated sharp cheddar cheese
4 eggs
2½ cups milk
½ teaspoon Dijon-style mustard
1 tablespoon minced fresh onion
½ teaspoon salt
A few dashes freshly ground black pepper

1. Coat a 1½-quart casserole dish with cooking spray.
2. Butter bread and cut into cubes. Place the cubes in the prepared dish. Top the bread cubes with 1 cup of cheddar cheese.
3. In a medium bowl, whisk eggs until well blended. Add milk, mustard, onion, salt, and pepper. Pour the mixture over the bread/cheese mixture. Top with remaining grated cheddar cheese. Cover and refrigerate overnight.
4. About 2 hours prior to cooking, remove casserole from refrigerator.
5. Preheat oven to 350°F.
6. Bake casserole uncovered for 1 hour. Serve immediately.

6 servings

Spicy Mediterranean Couscous with Beans and Vegetables

This is a striking and complementary combination. The sauce is very hot, so use it sparingly until you know its after-effects.

HOT SAUCE
½ cup olive oil
1 teaspoon cayenne pepper
2 tablespoons tomato paste
¼ cup fresh lime juice
½ teaspoon salt

COUSCOUS, BEANS AND VEGETABLES
1 box (5.6-ounces) couscous with toasted pine nuts
2 tablespoons neutral oil
1 large onion, chopped
1 red pepper, chopped into ½-inch dice
1 yellow pepper, cut into ½-inch dice
2 cans (14 ounces each) water-packed artichoke hearts, drained and quartered
2 cans (15 ounces each) garbanzo beans (chickpeas) with liquid
1 cup pitted and chopped Kalamata olives
1 tablespoon grated lemon peel
1 teaspoon fresh lemon juice
3 tablespoons minced fresh parsley

1. Preheat oven to 350°F.
2. To make the hot sauce, in a small bowl combine the olive oil with the cayenne pepper, tomato paste, lime juice, and salt. Whisk until mixture is blended. Set sauce aside. (The olive oil will naturally separate from the remaining ingredients; whisk again just before serving.)
3. Cook couscous according to package directions.
4. While the couscous is cooking, heat oil over moderate heat in a large skillet and sauté onion with red and yellow peppers and cook until tender. Remove from heat and add artichoke hearts, 1 can of garbanzo beans, olives, lemon peel, lemon juice, and parsley. Stir well to distribute ingredients evenly.
5. Combine remaining can of garbanzo beans with cooked couscous. Transfer this couscous/bean mixture to a lightly oiled 13 x 9 x 2-inch baking dish. Top with the vegetable/artichoke mixture.

6. Cover and bake for 30-40 minutes or until heated through. Serve immediately with hot sauce on the side.

6 servings

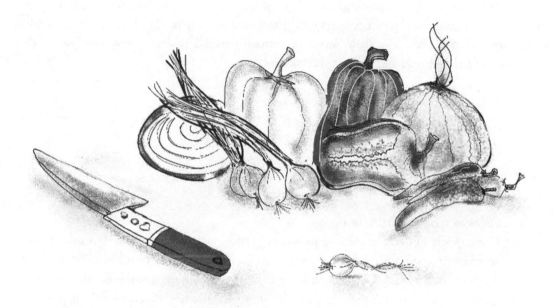

POLENTA WITH ROASTED PEPPERS, TOMATOES, AND CREAMY FONTINA

Polenta reigns supreme in northern Italy; it's even more popular than pasta! This casserole has been described as "exquisite comfort food." Any colored pepper works in this recipe, but I prefer to use yellow, orange and/or red peppers over green because they tend to be sweeter. I use Muir Glen tomatoes because I love their authentic tomato flavor. I typically serve this dish with a good-quality Italian bread and a leafy green salad.

3 large peppers
1 can (14.5 ounces) diced tomatoes
16 ounces polenta, cut into 16 slices
1¼ cup shredded Fontina cheese
Fresh basil leaves

1. Set oven temperature to broil.
2. Cut peppers in half and remove stems and seeds. Place pepper halves skin side up on a parchment-lined baking sheet. Flatten them using the palm of your hand. Broil peppers for 10 minutes or until blackened in spots. Remove from oven and place the peppers in a brown paper bag. Let peppers stand for about 15 minutes. Pull skin from peppers and cut into strips.
3. Set oven temperature to 350°F.
4. In a large bowl, combine peppers and tomatoes. Spoon half of the tomato/pepper mixture into a lightly oiled 13 x 9-inch baking dish. Top tomato/pepper mixture with half of the polenta slices. Repeat with the tomato/pepper mixture and polenta. Top the dish with cheese.
5. Bake uncovered for 25 minutes or until bubbly.
6. Set oven temperature to broil and broil for 1-2 minutes to lightly brown the cheese.
7. Top with fresh basil leaves. Serve immediately.

6 servings

FUSILLI WITH SUN-DRIED TOMATOES, PINE NUTS, AND FETA

I love how the fusilli catches all the ingredients in this delicious pasta dish. If you want a really pronounced tomato flavor, marinate the tomatoes overnight. To round out this meal, serve with a leafy green salad and slices of warm, crusty bread.

½ cup sun-dried tomatoes
1 cup boiling water
¼ cup olive oil
1 cup thinly sliced leeks
4 cloves garlic, thinly sliced
2 tablespoons small capers
⅓ cup toasted pine nuts
½ teaspoon salt
Freshly ground black pepper, to taste
Feta cheese, crumbled
½ pound (3 cups dry) fusilli pasta

1. In a small bowl, combine sun-dried tomatoes with 1 cup boiling water. Cover and let stand for 15 minutes or overnight. Remove tomatoes, reserving water, and cut into small pieces.
2. Bring a large pot of water to a boil. Cook fusilli according to package directions.
3. While the pasta is cooking, heat the oil in a sauté pan over moderate heat and sauté leeks until tender. Add garlic and cook for a few minutes.
4. Add tomato water, tomatoes, capers, pine nuts, salt, and pepper to the leek/garlic combination and stir to combine.
5. Divide pasta among 4 serving bowls and spoon tomato mixture over hot cooked pasta, distributing evenly. Serve immediately and pass the feta cheese to your guests.

4 servings

SPICY SPINACH AND POLENTA LASAGNA

A simple weeknight meal even the kids will love!

1¼ cups ricotta cheese
½ teaspoon crushed red pepper or to taste
1 teaspoon dried basil
½ teaspoon salt
Freshly ground black pepper, to taste
10 ounces frozen chopped spinach, defrosted, drained, and squeezed dry
½ cup freshly grated Parmesan cheese
16 ounces polenta, cut into 16 slices
1½ cups marinara sauce

1. Preheat oven to 350°F.
2. Coat a 13 x 9-inch baking dish with cooking spray.
3. In a medium bowl, combine ricotta cheese, red pepper, basil, salt, and pepper. Add spinach and ¼ cup of Parmesan cheese and mix until evenly distributed.
4. Spoon ¾ cup of marinara sauce over the bottom of the baking dish.
5. Arrange eight of the polenta slices over the sauce. Dollop half of the ricotta/spinach mixture over the polenta slices. (Don't worry about perfection because the mixture will even out during the baking process.)
6. Repeat with the remaining polenta slices. Top the slices with the remaining ricotta/spinach mixture.
7. Top with remaining ¾ cup of marinara sauce and top the sauce with ¼ cup Parmesan cheese.
8. Cover and bake for 30 minutes. Remove cover, switch oven temperature to broil to allow top to brown. Serve immediately.

4 to 6 servings

SPINACH AND MUSHROOM LOAF

This is a vegetarian "meatloaf" with spinach and mushrooms being the primary ingredients. My favorite accompaniments are slices of summer tomatoes, Orange Marmalade Tomatoes, or Curried Tomato Casserole (see Index for recipes).

2 tablespoons butter
1½ cups chopped onion
3 cloves garlic, minced
1 package (8 ounces) mushrooms, chopped
16 ounces frozen chopped spinach, defrosted, drained, and squeezed dry
¼ cup white wine
½ teaspoon ground cumin
2 teaspoons dried oregano
2 tablespoons soy sauce or tamari
1 cup ground almonds
½ cup dry bread crumbs
2 eggs

1. Preheat oven to 350°F.
2. In a large skillet over moderate heat, melt butter and sauté onions, garlic, and mushrooms until soft. Remove from heat and stir in spinach, wine, cumin, oregano, and soy sauce or tamari.
3. In a large bowl, combine almonds and bread crumbs. Add eggs and whisk until ingredients are well blended. Add mushroom mixture to bread crumb mixture and combine well.
4. Transfer mixture to an 11 x 7-inch baking dish and shape into a loaf. Bake for 30 minutes or until brown. Serve immediately.

4 to 6 servings

SUMMERTIME TOMATO PIE

Once summer rounds the corner, thoughts of eating juicy, garden-fresh tomatoes begin to enter my mind. Nothing compares to a ripe summer tomato. I can hardly wait (never buying the flavorless version from the grocery store) until they come into season when Nick and I go on a tomato-eating binge. Prepare Homemade Pie Crust (see page 132) or if crunched for time, buy a good-quality, frozen 9-inch pie shell.

½ cup mayonnaise
½ cup freshly grated Parmesan cheese
2 tablespoons white wine
½ teaspoon dry mustard
½ teaspoon garlic powder
½ teaspoon salt
¼ teaspoon cracked black pepper
2 tablespoons fresh minced parsley
1 (9-inch) baked pie crust
3-4 medium tomatoes, sliced (enough to fill the pie ¾ full)
15-20 fresh basil leaves

1. Preheat oven to 350°F.
2. In a medium bowl, combine mayonnaise with ¼ cup Parmesan cheese, white wine, dry mustard, garlic powder, salt, pepper, and parsley. Set mixture aside.
3. Arrange half of the tomatoes in the baked pie shell. Top the tomatoes with fresh basil leaves and top the basil leaves with remaining tomato slices.
4. Dollop the Parmesan/mayonnaise mixture over tomatoes. (Don't worry about perfection as the mixture will even out while baking.)
5. Top the pie with the remaining ¼ cup Parmesan cheese. Bake for 35-45 minutes or until lightly brown and bubbly. Serve immediately.

4 to 6 servings

TAMALE PIE

Tamale Pie is seasoned ground beef that is covered with a cornbread topping. There are many variations of this Mexican favorite. I'm especially wedded to this rendition because the cornbread part includes the same ingredients that are used in my popular recipe for Moist and Rich Chili Cornbread (see page 126). When our nephew Travis was visiting one summer, I prepared this dish. My plan was to serve it for dinner and have what was left over for another meal, but Travis ate the whole pie! I use Amy's Organic Cream of Tomato Soup in this recipe because I love the rich tomato flavor.

TAMALE PIE FILLING

1¼ pounds ground chuck
2 teaspoons chili powder
1 can (14.1 ounces) tomato soup
1 cup chopped red peppers
1 cup mild salsa
½ cup water

CORNBREAD TOPPING

2 eggs
1½ cups fresh corn kernels or frozen kernels
1 cup corn flour
2 teaspoons salt
3 teaspoons baking powder
1 cup sour cream
⅓ cup olive oil
1 cup shredded Monterey Jack cheese
1 can (4 ounces) chopped green chilies

1. Preheat oven to 350°F.
2. To prepare the filling, sauté ground chuck with chili powder in a large skillet over moderate heat and cook until meat is brown. Stir in tomato soup, peppers, salsa, and water. Bring mixture to a boil, decrease heat to simmer and cook for about 5 minutes. Transfer tamale pie filling to a 13 x 9 x 2-inch baking dish.
3. To prepare the cornbread topping, whisk eggs until well blended in a large bowl. Add corn kernels, corn flour, salt, baking powder, sour cream, olive oil, Monterey Jack cheese, and chilies. Spread cornbread mixture evenly over tamale pie.
4. Bake for 45 minutes. Serve immediately.

6 to 8 servings

Braised Beef Brisket

This brisket recipe promises to be one your guests will not soon forget. The method of covering the meat with lemon slices (a meat tenderizer) and onions, and cooking it for several hours at a low temperature turns out the most tender meat. Then it gets flooded with a bold-flavored sauce. So pronounced is the flavor of this entrée, I recommend serving it with unembellished accompaniments like steamed green beans and boiled potatoes. The brisket has to be cooked the day before you plan to serve it.

5 pounds brisket (weighed after the butcher has trimmed off the fat)
3-4 lemons, thinly sliced, seeds removed
Sliced onions, enough to cover the brisket
2 cups ketchup
2 cups water
2 teaspoons Worcestershire sauce
2 teaspoons Liquid Smoke
2 teaspoons packed brown sugar
1 teaspoon salt
A few dashes of Tabasco sauce or hot pepper sauce

1. Preheat oven to 250°F.
2. Place meat in a 15 x 10½-inch (4-liter) baking dish. Cover the brisket with lemon slices. Top the lemon slices with the onion slices. Cover with aluminum foil and bake for 6 hours.
3. When brisket has cooled, drain the essence from the meat and discard lemon and onion slices. Cover and refrigerate overnight.
4. In a large bowl, combine ketchup, water, Worcestershire sauce, Liquid Smoke, brown sugar, salt, and Tabasco or hot pepper sauce. Cover and set aside.
5. Remove the brisket from the refrigerator and allow it to come to room temperature. Thinly slice the meat against the grain. (Check the meat for lines that are running in the same direction; this is the grain. Position the knife perpendicular to the grain and thinly slice the brisket.)
6. Preheat oven to 350°F.
7. Pour the sauce over the brisket slices. Cover and bake for 1 hour. Serve immediately.

12 servings

MARINATED BEEF TENDERLOIN

This is one of the most requested entrées from catering clients and with good reason; it's a memorable, fork-tender piece of beef. It's got a multitude of flavorful ingredients and a lengthy marinating time—24 hours.

PINEAPPLE MARINADE

6 pounds beef tenderloin (trimmed and tied)
1 teaspoon salt
Several grindings of fresh black pepper
1 teaspoon Dijon-style mustard
¼ cup apple cider vinegar
¾ cup olive oil
1 cup pineapple juice

SAVORY AND SWEET RUB

½ cup packed brown sugar
4½ teaspoons celery seed
1½ teaspoons black pepper
3 teaspoons dry mustard
3 teaspoons salt
½ teaspoon paprika

BBQ SAUCE

3 tablespoons packed brown sugar
1½ teaspoons dry mustard
¾ teaspoon salt
½ teaspoon black pepper
2 tablespoons Worcestershire sauce
⅛ cup seasoned rice vinegar
¼ cup fresh lemon juice
1½ cups ketchup
1 tablespoon neutral oil
1 cup chopped onion

1. Place tenderloin in a baking dish large enough to hold the beef.
2. To make the pineapple marinade, combine the salt, pepper, mustard, and vinegar in a 3-cup jar with a tight-fitting lid. Shake contents until well combined. Add olive oil and shake until incorporated. Add pineapple juice. Pour marinade over tenderloin.

3. To make the savory and sweet rub, in a medium bowl combine the brown sugar with the celery seed, black pepper, dry mustard, salt, and paprika. Cover the top of the tenderloin with half of the dry rub mixture. Cover tenderloin and refrigerate.

4. About 12 hours later, turn tenderloin and cover the top with the remaining dry rub mixture.

5. To make the BBQ sauce, in a medium bowl combine the brown sugar, dry mustard, salt, and black pepper. Add Worcestershire sauce, rice vinegar, lemon juice, and ketchup, then whisk until well combined.

6. In a large skillet, heat oil over medium heat and sauté onion until slightly brown. Add BBQ sauce and whisk until well combined. Decrease heat to simmer and cook for about 15 minutes. Set BBQ sauce aside.

7. Remove tenderloin from refrigerator about 2 hours prior to cooking.

8. Preheat oven to 400°F.

9. Line a rimmed baking sheet with parchment paper overlapping the sides of the baking sheet. Drain marinade from the tenderloin and transfer it to the prepared baking sheet. Pour BBQ sauce over tenderloin and cook according to desired doneness.

10. Once cooked, immediately transfer tenderloin to a rimmed baking dish and allow meat to stand for at least 1 hour prior to slicing.

10 to 12 servings (1-1½ inch thick medallions)

TENDERLOIN COOKING CHART
Very rare: 35 minutes
Rare: 40-45 minutes
Medium rare: 50 minutes
Medium: 55-60 minutes

FILET OF BEEF WITH BACON, BLUE CHEESE, AND SUN-DRIED TOMATO STUFFING

This is one of Nick's all-time favorite recipes. It's also the entrée he has dubbed, "Invite-friends-for-dinner." Any spinach, tomato, or potato dish is an appropriate accompaniment.

4 beef filets (6-8 ounces each)
5 bacon slices, cut into 1-inch pieces
1 cup chopped onion
⅓ cup chopped sun-dried tomatoes
1 teaspoon dried rosemary, crushed
1 teaspoon dried basil
⅔ cup plain corn flakes, crushed
¾ cup crumbled blue cheese

1. Preheat oven to 375°.
2. With a sharp knife, slice each filet horizontally, being careful not to cut through to the other side.
3. In a sauté pan over medium heat, cook the bacon and onion for about 5 minutes. Add sun-dried tomatoes and cook until bacon and onion are lightly brown. Drain off any excess fat. Transfer bacon mixture to a medium bowl and add rosemary, basil, corn flakes, and blue cheese. Toss until well combined and ingredients look evenly distributed.
4. Pack about a ½ cup of stuffing into each filet (some stuffing mixture will billow out) and place stuffed filets on a parchment-lined baking sheet.
5. Cook for 5-7 minutes on each side or until desired doneness. Serve immediately.

4 servings

BROILED ORIENTAL FLANK STEAK

Flank steak only takes a few minutes to cook in the oven or on the grill, so I often find myself preparing this in the summer months when I don't want to heat up the kitchen. Appropriate accompaniments to this flavorful steak are Marinated Potato Salad and slices of summer tomatoes. But it's just as tasty when the weather turns colder, and I like to complement the steak with Creamy Mashed Potatoes and Orange Marmalade Tomatoes (see Index for recipes).

¼ cup cooking sherry
¼ cup soy sauce
¼ cup honey
2 tablespoons white vinegar
1 tablespoon minced fresh gingerroot, or 1 teaspoon ground ginger
1 teaspoon toasted sesame oil
2 cloves garlic, crushed
1¼ pound flank steak

1. In a baking dish large enough to accommodate the steak, combine the sherry, soy sauce, honey, vinegar, gingerroot or ground ginger, sesame oil, and garlic. Place the steak in the marinade, turning to coat. Cover and refrigerate for about 8 hours. Every few hours, turn steak to marinate evenly.
2. Allow the steak to come to room temperature before cooking.
3. Set oven temperature to broil.
4. Drain marinade from steak. Place steak on a rack and broil anywhere from 3-8 minutes on each side, depending on your desired preference of doneness. Let the steak rest for about 5 minutes. Cut the steak against the grain into thin slices. Serve immediately.

4 servings

CHILI RELLENOS CASSEROLE

This hearty, Mexican comfort food needs nothing more than a tossed lettuce leaf salad to accompany.

> *½ pound ground chuck*
> *1 cup chopped onion*
> *1½ teaspoons dried oregano*
> *½ teaspoon garlic powder*
> *¼ teaspoon salt*
> *A few grindings of fresh black pepper*
> *1 can (16 ounces) refried beans*
> *2 cans (4 ounces each) chopped green chilies*
> *1 cup shredded Monterey Jack cheese*
> *1 cup corn kernels*
> *3 eggs*
> *⅓ cup unbleached all-purpose flour*
> *1⅓ cups milk*
> *¼ teaspoon salt*
> *⅛ teaspoon Tabasco sauce or hot pepper sauce*
> *Sides of salsa, sour cream, and guacamole (see page 3 for guacamole recipe)*

1. Preheat oven to 350°F.
2. In a large skillet over medium heat, cook ground chuck and onion until brown. Drain off fat. Add oregano, garlic powder, salt, pepper, and refried beans to the beef mixture.
3. Line the bottom of an 11 x 7-inch baking dish with one can of the chopped green chilies. Top the green chilies with ½ cup of the cheese and spoon beef/bean mixture over cheese, leaving a ¼-inch border around the edge of the baking dish.
4. Distribute corn kernels and remaining can of chopped green chilies over beef/bean mixture. Top beef/bean mixture with remaining ½ cup of cheese.
5. In a large bowl, whisk eggs until well blended. Add flour and whisk until combined. Add milk, salt, and Tabasco or hot pepper sauce, and whisk until well blended. Pour mixture over casserole.
6. Bake uncovered for 1 hour. Serve immediately and pass the sides of salsa, sour cream, and guacamole to your guests.

6 servings

Beef Pot Roast

When the leaves on the trees mimic the colors that are so representative of the fall season, and the first sign of cold weather rounds the corner, beef pot roast is always on my list to prepare. Once the roast is in the oven I snuggle up in front of our fireplace and reduce my reading pile a few inches. While languishing, I enjoy the aroma that wafts from our kitchen stove and fills our house with the smell of a home-cooked meal. This beef pot roast recipe includes turnips and parsnips, some of autumn and winter's hearty, nutrient-rich root vegetables. Sweet Potato Biscuits or Buttermilk Biscuits (see Index for recipes) are delicious for sopping up the seasoned broth. If you choose to make Buttermilk Biscuits, they need to be prepared a day in advance. I use Imagine Brand Organic Free Range Chicken Broth and Muir Glen Tomatoes in this recipe because I love their authentic flavors.

4 pounds beef chuck roast
1 garlic clove, crushed
Unbleached all-purpose flour
Neutral oil
1 teaspoon salt
½ teaspoon black pepper
4 cups chicken broth
2-3 medium onions, quartered
1 can (28 ounces) whole tomatoes with juice
4-6 small to medium red or white potatoes, quartered
6-8 carrots, cut on the diagonal in pieces that are 2-3 inches long
3 small turnips, peeled and quartered
4 parsnips, peeled cut on the diagonal in pieces that are 2-3 inches long
3-4 stalks celery, cut in pieces that are 4-5 inches long

1. Preheat oven to 325°F.
2. Rub roast with garlic and dredge in flour, coating all sides of the roast.
3. Cover the bottom of a large skillet with oil and heat over moderately high heat. Brown meat on all sides. Transfer meat to a Dutch oven or a large roasting pan that is large enough to accommodate the meat plus all the vegetables. Season the roast with 1 teaspoon salt and black pepper. Pour the chicken broth over the roast and add the onions and tomatoes. Cover and cook for 1 hour.
4. Add potatoes, carrots, turnips, parsnips, and celery to the roast and cook for another 2-3 hours. (Turn the vegetables once or twice during that time to assure even cooking.)
5. Transfer roast to a deep serving platter and arrange vegetables around the roast. Spoon some of the essence over all. Serve immediately and pass additional essence in a gravy boat.

6 servings

SIMPLE CHILI

This crowd-pleasing hearty dish packs a lot of flavor with minimal preparation. In about one hour you can have a delicious pot of chili that tastes like it has been simmering for hours. I serve this with my recipe for Moist and Rich Chili Cornbread (see page 126). Tortilla chips are also a delicious accompaniment and can be used as a vessel to load chili onto. I serve the chili with sides of sour cream, shredded cheddar cheese, and lots of freshly chopped white onion.

1 pound ground chuck
1 medium onion, chopped
1 tablespoon chili powder
1 tablespoon Old Bay seasoning
½ teaspoon garlic powder
1 teaspoon Worcestershire sauce
2 cups tomato sauce
2 cans (15 ounces each) kidney beans
1 can (16 ounces) whole tomatoes
Sides of sour cream, shredded cheddar cheese, and freshly chopped white onion

1. In a large pot over moderate heat, cook the ground chuck. Add the onion and sauté until tender. Drain off fat. Stir in the chili powder, Old Bay seasoning, garlic powder, Worcestershire sauce, tomato sauce, kidney beans, and tomatoes. Cover and bring to a boil, decrease heat to medium-low and cook for 1 hour.
2. Serve immediately and pass sides of sour cream, cheddar cheese, and chopped onion to your guests.

6 servings

GINGER-GLAZED CHICKEN

This is a simple chicken entrée that's packed with flavor. Any leftover chicken can be sliced and turned into a delicious chicken sandwich.

½ cup Dijon-style mustard
¼ cup packed brown sugar
¼ cup honey
2 tablespoons minced fresh ginger
8 chicken cutlets, 2½-3 pounds

1. Preheat oven to 375°F.
2. In a medium bowl, combine mustard, brown sugar, honey, and ginger. Whisk until well blended.
3. Line a rimmed baking sheet with parchment paper. Coat the paper with cooking spray.
4. Place the cutlets on the prepared paper and brush both sides of the chicken with the mustard mixture. Spoon any extra sauce evenly over cutlets.
5. Bake for about 15 minutes on each side. Set oven temperature to broil and broil for 1-2 minutes on each side or until golden and slightly blackened. Serve immediately.

8 servings

CREAMY CHICKEN AND ZUCCHINI CASSEROLE WITH HERB STUFFING

A one-dish crowd-pleaser even kids love. It's a great choice for entertaining because it can be prepared in advance. Just pop it in the oven when the guests arrive or just prior to their arrival. I like to serve it with the Bloody Mary Aspic (see page 111). I use Amy's Cream of Mushroom Soup in this recipe because I like its chock-full-of-mushroom flavor. For the stuffing, I use a variety of breads that I've stockpiled in the freezer. Once the bread has thawed, I cube it and bake it in a 200°F oven until it's dry and crispy. You can use store-bought stuffing as well.

5 cups unpeeled medium zucchini, quartered and cut into ½-inch pieces
1 tablespoon neutral oil
1 cup finely chopped onion
1 cup chopped red or green pepper
5 cups bite-sized pieces of cooked chicken
1 can (14.1 ounce) cream of mushroom soup
1 cup sour cream
4 tablespoons butter
4 cups stuffing
1 cup chicken broth
1 cup shredded sharp cheddar cheese

1. Preheat oven to 350°F.
2. In a large pot, steam zucchini for about 5 minutes or until tender-crisp. Remove from heat and transfer zucchini to a rimmed baking dish to cool.
3. In a medium sauté pan, heat oil over moderate heat and sauté onion and peppers until tender. Transfer onions and peppers to a large bowl and add zucchini, chicken, mushroom soup, and sour cream. Combine until ingredients are evenly distributed.
4. In a large pot over low heat, melt butter. Remove from heat and add stuffing and chicken broth. Toss until the mixture is well combined. Transfer half of the stuffing mixture to a 13 x 9-inch baking dish, and reserve the rest for the top of the casserole.
5. Top stuffing mixture with zucchini/chicken mixture.
6. Top zucchini mixture with grated cheese and top cheese with remaining stuffing mixture.
7. Bake uncovered for 1 hour. Serve immediately.

10 servings

SPINACH-STUFFED CHICKEN BREASTS

When catering clients request chicken, I often suggest this recipe because it's unique and so flavorful. The key to making the flavor memorable will come from your generous hand when seasoning. This dish is delicious served with my recipe for Brandied Carrots with Peas (see page 90) and white rice that you've added a bit of wild rice to.

1 egg
20 ounces frozen chopped spinach, defrosted, drained, and squeezed dry
15 ounces ricotta cheese
¼ cup minced fresh parsley
¼ teaspoon salt
⅛ teaspoon nutmeg
1 tablespoon butter
1 medium onion, chopped (about 1 cup)
8 chicken breasts, bone in, skin on
Dijon-style mustard
Dried basil
Dried oregano
Paprika
Several grindings of fresh black pepper

1. Preheat oven to 350°F.
2. In a large bowl, beat egg with a wire whisk. Add spinach, ricotta, parsley, salt, and nutmeg. Set aside.
3. In a medium sauté pan, melt butter over moderate heat and sauté onion until translucent. Remove from heat and add onion to spinach/ricotta mixture. Stir until well blended.
4. Place chicken breasts in a single layer in a glass baking dish. Gently lift the skin from each chicken breast and stuff with the spinach/ricotta mixture, evenly distributing the mixture across the top of the breast. Gently pull the skin over the chicken to cover the breast. (No place for perfection here, so don't worry if some of the mixture isn't covered with the skin.)
5. Spread a generous amount of mustard evenly over each chicken breast and liberally season with basil, oregano, and paprika. Lightly season with black pepper.
6. Bake uncovered for 1 hour (or more) or until chicken is cooked through.
7. When chicken breasts are cool enough to handle, carefully remove the bone. (Reserve the chicken bones for making chicken stock.) Don't worry if some of the seasoning comes off from handling the breasts.
8. Serve de-boned chicken breasts as they are, or slice the breasts about a half-inch thick. (It's a matter of preference.) Either way, serve them warm. Place them back in the baking dish, cover and warm them in a 200°F oven until heated through.

8 servings

Soba Noodle Salad with Pears and Pork

With an abundance of flavor and texture, this main entrée always pleases, even those who have traditional palates. This recipe uses the Sesame Pork Tenderloin recipe (see page 80). You only need one of the tenderloins; reserve the other for another meal. If you're not familiar, Soba noodles are native Japanese pasta made of buckwheat and wheat flour.

3 tablespoons neutral oil
2 tablespoons toasted sesame oil
2 tablespoons soy sauce or tamari
2 tablespoons seasoned rice vinegar
4 teaspoons Dijon-style mustard
1 Sesame Pork Tenderloin (see page 80), sliced
1 package (8.8 ounce) Soba noodles, broken in half
½ cup sliced scallions (green onions), white and green part
1 red pepper, diced
2 Asian pears, cut into bite-sized pieces
2 tablespoons toasted sesame seeds

1. In a medium bowl, combine oil, dark sesame oil, soy sauce or tamari, vinegar, and mustard. Whisk until well combined.
2. Cook noodles according to package directions. Transfer noodles to a large serving bowl and allow them to cool.
3. Pour dressing over the noodles and add scallions and red pepper, then toss to combine. Marinate at room temperature for about 2 hours.
4. Divide noodles among six shallow serving bowls. Top the noodles with slices of tenderloin, pears, and sesame seeds. Serve immediately.

6 servings

SESAME PORK TENDERLOIN WITH MUSTARD CREAM

In my opinion, Grey Poupon is not only a delicious condiment, but do you remember their hoity-toity commercials? Grey Poupon is the names of two 18th-century, big-time mustard firms from Dijon run by men named Maurice Grey and Antoine Poupon. Not surprisingly, Grey Poupon won a gold medal in the Dijon category at the Worldwide Mustard Competition at the Napa Valley Mustard Festival! I often serve this tenderloin with Brandied Carrots with Peas and Creamy Mashed Potatoes (see Index for recipes). For cream to whip properly, place the mixing bowl and/or beaters in the freezer for about 2 hours prior to preparing Mustard Cream.

SESAME PORK TENDERLOIN

½ cup soy sauce or tamari
3 tablespoons sugar
2 tablespoons minced onion
2 cloves garlic, minced
2 teaspoons ground ginger
¾ cup sesame seeds
2 pork tenderloins

MUSTARD CREAM

1 cup heavy whipping cream
⅓ cup Dijon-style mustard
1 tablespoon Worcestershire sauce

1. In a medium bowl, combine soy sauce or tamari, sugar, minced onion, garlic, ground ginger, and sesame seeds. Transfer mixture to a baking dish to accommodate all the ingredients. Add tenderloins and turn to coat on all sides. Cover and refrigerate. Marinate for about 3 hours.
2. Allow tenderloins to come to room temperature.
3. Preheat oven to 375°F.
4. Drain tenderloins and bake for 45 minutes. Allow tenderloins to cool for about 10 minutes before slicing.
5. Pour whipping cream into medium bowl and beat on medium speed. When the cream thickens, increase the speed and continue to beat until cream falls in large globs and has soft peaks. Fold in mustard and Worcestershire sauce. Serve immediately or refrigerate until ready to serve.
6. Serve sliced tenderloin and pass the Mustard Cream to your guests.

8 to 10 servings

BAKED HAM

When I was growing up, ham was frequently served because my mother loved it—and so did we! She liked that ham had so many endless possibilities for leftovers. Leftover ham was used in sandwiches, added to soups, casseroles, and savory pies. I serve this ham on special occasions and usually for Easter dinner. On those special occasions, I like to serve it with roasted asparagus, Carrot and Leek Gratin, Creamy Mashed Potatoes, and Honey-Glazed Pineapple (see Index for recipes). I use the leftover broth from the cooked ham as a foundation for bean soup.

1 butt end ham
1 cup chicken broth
1 cup white wine
2 stalks celery, cut into large chunks
2 medium carrots, peeled and cut into large chunks
2 medium onions, quartered

1. Preheat oven to 350°F.
2. Place the ham in a roasting pan and add chicken broth, wine, celery, carrots, and onions. Cover and bake for 1½-2 hours.
3. Transfer ham from the roasting pan to a platter. Set aside and allow ham to cool before carving.
4. Discard celery, carrots, and onions. Transfer broth to a container. When broth has cooled, cover and refrigerate. The following day, or before you use the broth, skim off any fat that has risen to the top.

Serves a crowd

Vegetables & potatoes

INTRODUCING VEGETABLE AND POTATO SIDE DISHES

I owe my love of vegetables to my mother. They always took center stage on our plates, and she made sure to bring out their flavor through the use of seasonings. For me, a meal isn't complete without complementing side dishes. There is lots of comfort food in this chapter, like Creamy Mashed Potatoes and Seasoned Vegetable Medley with Melted Cheese. My recipes for Orange Marmalade Tomatoes, Brandied Carrots with Peas, and Carrot and Leek Gratin round out a variety of entrees, and they're reliable when entertaining. I think you will find yourself coming back to them time and time again.

VEGETABLE SIDE DISHES

POTATOES

Seasoned Vegetable Medley Topped with Melted Cheese

In my early twenties, I worked in a restaurant owned by an energetic man named Harvey Shugarman. This gluten-free dish—gluten-free hadn't come into vogue yet—known as the Vegetarian Delight was among the most popular items on the menu with the getting-ready-to-fit-in-the-summer-wardrobe crowd.

I love its versatility; just about any vegetable works. If you don't have one of the vegetables called for in this recipe, be creative and design your own combination of vegetables. Offer slices of authentic French, Italian, or ciabatta bread with olive oil for dipping, or offer breadsticks to the getting-ready-to-fit-in-the-summer-wardrobe crowd, as was customary at Harvey's restaurant.

Hardier vegetables require longer cooking times than the more delicate ones. You don't want mushy vegetables, so it's important to cook vegetables until just fork-tender. The amount of Old Bay seasoning is a matter of preference. I tend to be heavy-handed because the seasoning is what brings all the flavors together. I prefer a variety of cheeses, and, like the versatility of the vegetables, just about any flavorful good-melting cheese works.

2 cups julienned carrots
2 cups bite-sized cauliflower florets
2 cups bite-sized broccoli florets
1½ cups quartered sliced zucchini, ½-inch pieces
2 cups yellow squash, ½-inch slices
2 cups sliced celery, ¼-inch slices
1 large onion cut into chunks
1 teaspoon Old Bay seasoning
⅓ cup freshly grated Parmesan cheese
2 cups shredded cheese like mozzarella, Monterey Jack, or sharp white cheddar

1. Set oven temperature to broil.
2. In a large pot with a steamer, bring water to a boil. Steam the carrots, cauliflower, and broccoli until not yet fork-tender. Keep these vegetables in the steamer and add the zucchini, yellow squash, celery, and onion. Cook until just fork-tender.
3. Carefully transfer the vegetables to a baking dish and gently toss them to evenly distribute. Season the vegetables with Old Bay seasoning. Top the vegetables with Parmesan and shredded cheeses.
4. Place baking dish under broiler and broil until cheese melts and turns a light golden brown. Serve immediately.

6 servings

CURRIED RICE
WITH MANGO AND CASHEWS

This delightful-tasting side dish is abundant with flavor, and I love the autumnal colors. I'm partial to mangoes because the taste of them resembles some of my favorite fruits—peaches, apricots, and pineapples. If you need instructions on how to ripen a mango and/or how to remove the flesh, go to the Product and Food Guide (see page 206). This dish is delicious with grilled or baked chicken.

1½ cups basmati rice
1 tablespoon neutral oil
1 tablespoon curry powder
1 teaspoon salt
2 cups bite-sized cauliflower florets
¼ cup dried cranberries
¼ cup water
½ cup cashews, toasted
1 cup ripe mango, peeled and cut into bite-sized pieces
3 tablespoons snipped fresh chives
¼ teaspoon black pepper

1. Cook basmati rice according to package directions.
2. While the rice is cooking, heat oil in a medium skillet over low heat. Add curry powder and cook for 1-2 minutes, until fragrant. Add the salt and cauliflower and stir until the curry powder adheres to the cauliflower. Add the dried cranberries and water and stir to combine. Cover and cook over low heat for 5-15 minutes until the cauliflower is just tender. Check every 5 minutes.
3. Transfer the cooked rice to a large bowl. Add cauliflower mixture and toss to combine. Add cashews, mangoes, chives and black pepper. Toss remaining ingredients until evenly distributed.
4. Cover and allow dish to stand at room temperature for at least a half-hour before serving.

6 servings

ORANGE MARMALADE TOMATOES

This is a popular tomato dish that you can rely on to serve for everyday eating or whenever you're entertaining. Serve with your favorite beef recipe or any of the beef recipes in this cookbook. Or, for a well-rounded, colorful, and complementary vegetarian meal, serve with Broccoli, Sweet Onion, and Cashew Salad and Savory Cheddar Cheese Casserole (see Index for recipes).

2 tablespoons butter
1 teaspoon curry powder
1 cup chopped onion
1 can (28 ounces) diced tomatoes
½ cup orange marmalade
1 teaspoon ground cinnamon
1 teaspoon salt
Several grindings of fresh black pepper

1. Preheat oven to 350°F.
2. Melt butter in a large sauté pan over moderate heat, then add curry powder. Stir for a minute or so or until fragrant. Add onion and sauté for about 5 minutes or until tender. Add tomatoes, orange marmalade, and cinnamon. Bring mixture to a boil, remove from heat, and season with salt and pepper.
3. Transfer mixture to a 2-liter baking dish. Bake uncovered for 45 minutes. Serve immediately.

6 servings

LAYERS OF SUMMER'S HARVEST

When potatoes, zucchini, and tomatoes are at the peak of their growing season, I often prepare this simple, colorful, tasty dish. It is delicious served with chicken, fish, meat, or pork, and I love it with scrambled eggs. Whatever you choose to serve with it, slices of good-quality bread are delicious accompaniments to dip into the seasoned essence that comes naturally from cooking the vegetables.

Olive oil
6 small to medium potatoes or about 1½ pounds, thinly sliced
2 medium zucchini, thinly sliced
3-4 ripe tomatoes, sliced
Coarse salt
Several grindings of freshly ground black pepper
3 cloves garlic, minced
Fresh minced parsley (garnish)

1. Preheat oven to 350°F.
2. Lightly oil a 9 x 13-inch baking dish with cooking spray.
3. Lay sliced potatoes in the bottom of the baking dish, overlapping the slices by half. Drizzle the potatoes with olive oil and season with salt and pepper.
4. Cover the potatoes with the zucchini slices overlapping by half. Drizzle the zucchini with olive oil and season with salt, pepper, and minced garlic.
5. Cover the zucchini with the tomato slices and drizzle with olive oil, salt, and pepper.
6. Cover and bake for 50-60 minutes or until potatoes are tender when pierced. Garnish with parsley. Serve immediately.

10 to 12 servings

BAKED SPINACH
WITH CHEESE

For an elegant and delicious meal, I like to serve this spinach dish with Marinated Beef Tenderloin or Broiled Oriental Flank Steak. Round out the meal with your favorite potato dish or Creamy Mashed Potatoes (see Index for recipes).

16 ounces frozen chopped spinach, defrosted, drained, and squeezed dry
1 cup finely chopped onion
½ cup crumbled feta cheese
½ cup grated Edam cheese
¼ cup crumbled blue cheese
¼ teaspoon ground nutmeg
2 tablespoons dry bread crumbs
3 tablespoons olive oil
2 tablespoons freshly grated Parmesan cheese

1. Preheat oven to 350°F.
2. Oil a 9-inch baking dish with cooking spray.
3. Arrange spinach in the bottom of the baking dish.
4. In a medium bowl, combine onion, feta, Edam, blue cheese, nutmeg, bread crumbs, and olive oil. Combine until well blended and evenly distributed.
5. Top spinach with cheese mixture and sprinkle with Parmesan.
6. Bake for 20-30 minutes. Switch oven temperature to broil and brown top. Serve immediately.

8 servings

Brandied Carrots
with Peas

This is one of those recipes I'm always drawn to serving because it's easy, colorful, crowd-pleasing, and goes with almost any entrée.

8 large carrots, peeled and cut into julienne strips
4 tablespoons butter
2 tablespoons sugar
½ teaspoon salt
⅓ cup brandy
1 cup frozen green peas, thawed

1. Preheat oven to 350°F.
2. Place carrots in a 2-quart baking dish.
3. In a medium saucepan, melt the butter over medium heat. Add sugar, salt, and brandy, then stir until sugar and salt dissolve. Pour the mixture over the carrots.
4. Cover and bake for 45 minutes or until carrots are tender.
5. When carrots emerge from the oven, add the peas and toss to combine. Serve immediately.

8 servings

CURRIED TOMATO CASSEROLE

This is as simple as it is tasty. The bread crumbs blend into the tomato mixture, turning out a creamy textured dish. I use Muir Glen tomatoes in this recipe because I love the rich, authentic tomato taste.

> *8 tablespoons (1 stick) butter*
> *1 large onion, chopped*
> *½ teaspoon curry powder*
> *2 cans (28 ounces each) diced tomatoes*
> *¼ cup sugar*
> *About 7 drops Tabasco sauce or hot pepper sauce*
> *1 teaspoon salt*
> *Several grindings of fresh black pepper*
> *1½ cups seasoned dry bread crumbs*

1. Preheat oven to 350°F.
2. Melt butter in a large sauté pan over medium heat. Sauté onion until tender. Add curry powder and cook for about 1 minute. Add tomatoes, sugar, Tabasco or hot pepper sauce, salt, and pepper. Stir until well combined.
3. Transfer mixture to a 2-liter baking dish. Top the tomatoes with the bread crumbs. Bake uncovered for 1 hour. Serve immediately.

8 to 10 servings

CARROT AND LEEK GRATIN

This is a delicious side dish that's extraordinarily popular. I rely on it whenever I'm hosting dinner parties. It complements just about any entrée. I've successfully served it with fish, beef, lamb, pork, and chicken. Five tablespoons of horseradish may seem excessive, but it's what gives this dish its memorable zesty flavor.

2 tablespoons butter
4 cups shredded carrots (about 6 medium carrots)
2 cups sliced leeks, white part only (4-5 medium leeks)
5 tablespoons prepared horseradish
1 teaspoon salt
A few grindings of fresh ground black pepper
1 cup heavy whipping cream
1 cup milk
2 eggs
⅓ cup dry bread crumbs
½ cup shredded white cheddar cheese

1. Preheat oven to 350°F.
2. Lightly oil a 2-quart baking dish with cooking spray.
3. In a large skillet over moderate heat, melt butter, then sauté carrots and leeks for 4-5 minutes until tender. Remove from heat and stir in horseradish, salt, and pepper. Transfer mixture to the prepared baking dish.
4. In a medium bowl, whisk together the cream, milk, and eggs. Pour the mixture over the carrot/leek mixture and lightly stir to evenly distribute.
5. Bake uncovered for 30 minutes.
6. In a small bowl, combine bread crumbs and cheese. Set mixture aside.
7. After 30 minutes, remove the gratin from the oven and top with the bread crumb/cheese mixture.
8. Bake uncovered for an additional 25 minutes. Serve immediately.

6 to 8 servings

CELERY AMANDINE

This is a unique side dish that beautifully complements baked chicken and steamed rice—a crowd-pleasing trio that will not disappoint.

2 tablespoons butter
⅓ cup slivered almonds
½ cup chicken broth
1 tablespoon dried minced onion
1 teaspoon garlic powder
1 teaspoon powdered ginger
2 teaspoons soy sauce or tamari
4 cups diagonally sliced celery, about ¼-inch thick

1. Melt butter in a medium sauté pan over moderate heat. Add the slivered almonds and sauté until light brown, stirring often. (Watch closely to make sure they don't burn.) Add chicken broth, dried minced onion, garlic powder, ginger, soy sauce or tamari, and celery. Stir to combine the ingredients.
2. Cover and decrease heat to medium-low and cook for 10-20 minutes or until celery is tender, stirring once or twice during the cooking process. Serve immediately.

4 servings

BOUNTIFUL POTATO SALAD

This recipe is great for summer potluck parties, picnics, or barbeques. It complements fish, barbecued chicken or ribs, and is also delicious with bean or beef burgers, as well as grilled steak.

2¼ pounds whole (about golf-ball sized) red potatoes, unpeeled
1¼ cups chopped celery
¼ cup small capers
½ cup Spanish green olives with pimentos, sliced into thirds
½ cup chopped scallions (green onions)
½ cup chopped sweet gherkins
3 chopped hard-boiled eggs
¾ cup mayonnaise
⅛ cup apple cider vinegar
1 tablespoon sugar
2 teaspoons Dijon-style mustard
1 tablespoon celery seed
Freshly ground black pepper, to taste

1. Place potatoes in a large pot, cover with cold water and place over medium-high heat. When water comes to a boil, cover, lower heat to medium (water should be dancing), and cook potatoes for 20-30 minutes, until fork-tender. Drain potatoes and allow them to cool completely. When cool enough to handle, cut potatoes into bite-sized pieces and place in a large bowl.
2. In a medium bowl, combine celery, capers, green olives, scallions, sweet gherkins, and eggs. Add to potatoes and gently toss.
3. In a medium bowl, combine mayonnaise, vinegar, sugar, mustard, celery seeds, and pepper. Whisk until smooth. Pour dressing over potato mixture and toss to combine. Cover and refrigerate for at least 2 hours before serving.

10 servings

Marinated Potato Salad

My mother has been preparing this potato salad since she and my father first ate it at a potluck picnic with friends in the summer of 1945. The woman who prepared the salad said it wasn't at all like traditional potato salad because it had a mere tablespoon of mayonnaise. (Mayonnaise was being rationed at the time, but potatoes and onions were plentiful and inexpensive.) So she decided to experiment and dress the potato salad with an oil and vinegar-based dressing rather than the traditional mayonnaise-based dressing. Everyone loved it! It's as popular and picnic-friendly now as it was then. It goes well with just about anything that goes with potatoes and especially anything from the grill.

The original recipe used apple cider vinegar, but I use seasoned rice vinegar—both make a great-tasting dressing. Peeling the potatoes is a matter of preference.

½ cup neutral oil
¼ cup seasoned rice vinegar
1 teaspoon celery seed
1 teaspoon salt
¾ teaspoon black pepper
6 medium potatoes, unpeeled, quartered
1½ cups quartered and thinly sliced onion
1 tablespoon mayonnaise

1. In a 1-cup jar with a tight-fitting lid, combine oil, vinegar, celery seed, salt, and pepper. Shake contents until well combined. Allow dressing to stand at room temperature for several hours.
2. Cook potatoes in boiling, salted water for about 15 minutes or until tender. Allow potatoes to cool. When cool enough to handle, thinly slice.
3. Layer the potatoes and the onions alternately in a rimmed dish large enough to accommodate the ingredients.
4. Shake dressing and pour evenly over the potatoes and onions. Cover and refrigerate for several hours or overnight. (Overnight is recommended.)
5. Just before serving, toss the salad with the mayonnaise. Season with additional salt if desired.

6 servings

BACON-STUFFED POTATOES

For even baking, choose potatoes that are uniform in size.

4 baking potatoes
½ cup sour cream
2 tablespoons butter, softened
¾ cup buttermilk
½ cup shredded white cheddar cheese
⅓ cup chopped scallions (green onions)
½ teaspoon salt or to taste
Several grindings of fresh black pepper
4 slices crispy cooked bacon

1. Preheat oven to 350°F.
2. Bake potatoes for 1 hour or until a fork slides easily through the center. When potatoes are cool enough to handle, cut them in half and scoop out the pulp. Place the pulp in a large bowl. Set the potato skins aside. Mash the potatoes.
3. In a large bowl, combine sour cream with softened butter. Whisk in buttermilk and add cheddar cheese, scallions, salt, pepper, and bacon. Combine mixture with the mashed potatoes and mix well. (For creamier potatoes, adjust the amounts of sour cream, butter, and/or buttermilk.) Spoon potato mixture into potato skins.
4. Place stuffed potatoes on a baking sheet and bake for 20-30 minutes or until heated through.
5. Adjust oven temperature to broil and lightly brown the top of potatoes. Serve immediately.

8 servings

CREAMY MASHED POTATOES

The best potatoes for mashing are russet, Yukon gold, or red potatoes. If potatoes seem like they need to be creamier, add some of the reserved potato water.

5 pounds potatoes, quartered (peeled if desired)
1 teaspoon salt
8 ounces cream cheese, softened
1 cup sour cream
2 tablespoons butter, softened
2 tablespoons dried minced onion
1 teaspoon salt
Several grindings of freshly ground black pepper

1. Fill a large pot with water. Add salt and bring the water to a boil. Add potatoes. Allow the water to return to a boil, cover and decrease heat to medium. Cook potatoes for 20-30 minutes or until fork-tender.
2. Drain potatoes, reserving some of the water, and transfer to a large bowl. Mash potatoes until almost creamy.
3. In a medium bowl, beat the cream cheese, sour cream, butter, minced onion, salt, and pepper until well blended. Add the cream mixture to the potatoes and beat (being careful not to over-beat) until ingredients are blended.
4. Season to taste with additional salt and pepper. Serve immediately.

12 servings

salads

INTRODUCING SEAFOOD SALADS, HEARTY VEGETABLE SALADS, AND WARM WEATHER SALADS

Whenever I design salad combinations, I focus on bringing together lots of colors, textures, and foods from different food groups. I especially love to add nuts, unusual vegetables, crumbly cheeses, and fresh and dried fruits to salads because they add such a depth of texture and flavor. This chapter offers many unique, crowd-pleasing recipes that often use a vast variety of all the foods I love in a salad.

During the summer months when tomatoes are at the height of their season, I rely on the seafood salad recipes whenever I'm entertaining or having a friend over for lunch. They're all colorful and refreshing—good hot weather fare. The hearty vegetable salads like Red Cabbage Salad with Mango, Avocado, Feta, and Cashews, and Hearts of Palm, Mango, and Cashew Salad with Salty Lime Dressing are examples of using a variety of ingredients with lots of contrasting textures.

I couldn't resist including the aspics because they accompanied so many luncheon platters in the 1950s, '60s and '70s not only because they were so trendy, but also because aspics are tasty and colorful fill-ins when you need a complementary cold salad and/or a colorful side dish. They can be prepared in advance, a feature I love when entertaining.

SEAFOOD SALADS

Greek Shrimp Salad with Lemon Dressing 101

Summer Tomato and Shrimp Salad 102

Curried Tuna Salad with Cranberries and Cashews 103

Basil-Drenched Fusilli Salad with Shrimp, Peas, and Heirloom Tomatoes 104

HEARTY VEGETABLE SALADS

Zesty Coleslaw with Peanuts 105

Broccoli, Sweet Onion, and Cashew Salad 106

Red Cabbage Salad with Cranberries, Walnuts, and Roquefort 107

Red Cabbage Salad with Mango, Avocado, Feta, and Cashews 108

Green Bean Salad with Gingered Walnuts, Cranberries, and Feta 109

WARM-WEATHER SALADS

Bloody Mary Aspic 111

Tomato Raspberry Aspic 112

Zucchini Salad with Warm Walnut Dressing 113

Iceberg Lettuce Stuffed with Blue Cheese Dressing 114

Hearts of Palm, Mango, and Cashew Salad with Salty Lime Dressing 115

GREEK SHRIMP SALAD WITH LEMON DRESSING

Our friend Jane Durkee prepared this for my husband and me one glorious summer Sunday. It tasted as wonderful as the day was beautiful. Delicious companions to this impressive meal are Moist and Rich Chili Cornbread (see page 126), or if you want a lighter accompaniment, serve with slices of ciabatta bread.

LEMON DRESSING
¼ cup fresh lemon juice
½ teaspoon dried oregano
½ teaspoon dried basil
1 clove garlic, crushed
½ cup olive oil
½ cup minced fresh parsley
½ teaspoon salt
Several grindings of fresh black pepper
2 pounds large cooked shrimp, peeled and deveined

SHRIMP SALAD
1 tablespoon neutral oil
½ teaspoon dried oregano
⅔ cup pecan halves
½ cup thinly sliced scallions (green onions)
¾ cup pitted and chopped Kalamata olives
6 servings of assorted lettuce leaves, torn into bite-sized pieces
2-3 medium tomatoes, cut into wedges
2 ripe avocados, cut into bite-sized pieces

1. To make the lemon dressing, combine the lemon juice, oregano, basil, garlic, olive oil, parsley, salt, and pepper in the bowl of a food processor fitted with a steel blade, then process until blended. Transfer dressing to a large bowl.
2. Add the shrimp and marinate it in the dressing for about 4 hours.
3. In a medium skillet, heat oil over moderate heat and sauté oregano and pecans until pecans are lightly browned. Set aside.
4. In a large bowl, toss scallions, olives, and lettuce leaves with enough marinade to coat the leaves. Divide lettuce leaves among 6 serving plates and distribute shrimp evenly over salad.
5. Arrange tomato wedges and avocado on top of salad. Top salad with seasoned pecans. Serve immediately.

6 servings

SUMMER TOMATO
AND SHRIMP SALAD

This is a great dish to serve for a summer luncheon or supper. Serve this salad with your favorite bread; I like a good-quality French or Italian.

½ teaspoon celery seed
1 teaspoon salt
1 teaspoon sugar
Several grindings of fresh black pepper
¼ cup white wine vinegar
1 clove garlic, minced
1 teaspoon Worcestershire sauce
¼ cup olive oil
¼ cup neutral oil
2 pounds cooked shrimp, peeled and deveined
2 medium ripe tomatoes, cut into chunks
1 medium sweet onion, cut into bite-sized pieces
6 generous handfuls of assorted lettuce leaves

1. In a large bowl, combine celery seed, salt, sugar, pepper, vinegar, garlic, and Worcestershire sauce. Slowly add oils to vinegar mixture and whisk until well blended.
2. Toss shrimp with dressing. Transfer shrimp to a large rimmed serving platter and gently toss with tomatoes and onions.
3. Divide lettuce leaves among 6 rimmed serving bowls. Evenly distribute shrimp combination over lettuce leaves. Serve immediately.

6 servings

CURRIED TUNA SALAD
WITH CRANBERRIES AND CASHEWS

The testers who tasted this salad described it as extraordinarily flavorful, and everyone loved the contrasting textures. I suggest serving it with authentic ciabatta. I like to accompany this dish with slices of summer tomatoes and deviled eggs. The amount of olive oil may seem excessive, especially when you first toss it with the salad ingredients. (It might seem like one of those salads you got in a restaurant that was swimming in dressing). But not to worry—the dressing tends to be absorbed quickly, and what remains allows the bread to serve its purpose. My preferred choice of lettuce leaves is either Bibb or Boston; the shape is perfect and sturdy enough to hold the salad.

CURRY DRESSING
1 cup olive oil
½ cup fresh lemon juice
2 cloves garlic, minced
2 teaspoons curry powder
1 teaspoon ginger
1 teaspoon salt
¼-½ teaspoon pepper

TUNA SALAD
4 cans (5 ounces each) solid white tuna packed in water, drained and flaked
⅓ cup dried cranberries
⅔ cup roasted, salted cashews, chopped
½ cup thinly sliced scallions (green onions)
Bibb or Boston lettuce leaves

1. In a large bowl, combine olive oil, lemon juice, garlic, curry powder, ginger, salt, and pepper. Whisk until well blended.
2. In a large bowl, toss tuna with cranberries, cashews, and scallions. Toss tuna mixture with curry dressing.
3. Divide lettuce leaves among 8 rimmed serving plates and top lettuce with tuna salad. Serve immediately.

8 servings

BASIL-DRENCHED FUSILLI SALAD WITH SHRIMP, PEAS, AND HEIRLOOM TOMATOES

Some describe fusilli as "twisted spaghetti," but fusilli is actually a helix. Whatever it's called, I love the way it catches the basil dressing in this recipe. For optimum flavor, prepare this dish during the summer months when basil and tomatoes are at the peak of their growing season.

3 cups fresh basil leaves
½ cup olive oil
¼ cup seasoned rice vinegar
½ teaspoon salt
Several grindings of fresh black pepper
½ pound fusilli, cooked according to package directions and cooled
2 pounds large cooked shrimp, peeled and deveined
2 cups frozen peas, thawed
2 large heirloom tomatoes, cut into bite-sized pieces

1. Drop basil leaves into the bowl of a food processor fitted with a steel blade, then add olive oil, vinegar, salt, and fresh ground black pepper. Process until well blended.
2. In a large bowl, combine fusilli with shrimp, peas, and tomatoes. Toss with basil dressing. Serve immediately.

6 servings

ZESTY COLESLAW
WITH PEANUTS

This coleslaw gets its lively flavor from a generous seasoning of cayenne pepper.

ZESTY DRESSING
1 cup plain yogurt
1 cup mayonnaise
1 tablespoon toasted sesame oil
¼ cup apple cider vinegar
½ cup chopped red onion
1 teaspoon celery seed
½ teaspoon cayenne pepper, or to taste
½ teaspoon black pepper
1 teaspoon salt
1 tablespoon sugar

COLESLAW
10-12 cups shredded Savoy cabbage
10-12 cups shredded red cabbage
6 carrots, peeled and shredded
1 cup peanuts, roasted

1. In a food processor, combine the yogurt, mayonnaise, sesame oil, vinegar, and red onion. Purée until smooth. Add the celery seed, cayenne pepper, black pepper, salt, and sugar, then blend until all ingredients are incorporated. Transfer to a container, cover, and refrigerate overnight.
2. In a large bowl, toss Savoy cabbage with red cabbage and carrots. Pour dressing over mixture and toss until dressing is well combined with cabbage. Top with peanuts. Serve immediately.

Serves a crowd

Broccoli, Sweet Onion, and Cashew Salad

This is a gorgeous celebration of colors that is as delicious as it is beautiful. It's the perfect accompaniment to fish, chicken or beef. Cook the broccoli until just fork-tender because under-cooked or over-cooked broccoli (there is a narrow window) will result in a completely different salad—one that is mushy.

DRESSING
1 clove garlic, minced
1 tablespoon seasoned rice vinegar
1 tablespoon olive oil
1 tablespoon mayonnaise
1 teaspoon sugar
1 teaspoon tamari or soy sauce
Several grindings of fresh black pepper

SALAD
3 cups bite-sized broccoli florets
½ cup thinly sliced sweet onion (Vidalia, etc.)
½ cup chopped red pepper
½ cup roasted, salted cashew pieces
¼ cup dried cranberries

1. To prepare the dressing, whisk the garlic, vinegar, olive oil, mayonnaise, sugar, tamari or soy sauce, and black pepper in a small bowl until well blended. Set dressing aside.
2. Place a shallow rimmed bowl or platter in the refrigerator to chill while the broccoli is cooking—this will keep the broccoli from cooking more after it has been transferred from the steamer.
3. Steam broccoli until just fork-tender. Transfer it to the chilled bowl or platter and keep at room temperature. Add the onion and red pepper to the broccoli.
4. To assemble the salad, pour the dressing over the broccoli mixture and gently toss until well combined. Add cashews and cranberries. Serve immediately.

4 servings

RED CABBAGE SALAD WITH CRANBERRIES, WALNUTS, AND ROQUEFORT

Fair warning, this is a popular salad.

Prepare Celery Seed Dressing *(see page 137)*

5 cups shredded red cabbage
⅓ cup dried cranberries
⅓ cup coarsely chopped walnuts, toasted
⅓ cup thinly sliced scallions (green onions)
½ cup crumbled Roquefort cheese

1. In a large bowl, combine cabbage, cranberries, walnuts, scallions, and Roquefort. Toss with just enough dressing to coat the ingredients. Season with salt and pepper. Serve immediately.

4 to 6 servings

RED CABBAGE SALAD WITH MANGO, AVOCADO, FETA, AND CASHEWS

If you're looking to prepare a salad with lots of flavor, color, and texture, you have met your match with this delicious combination—so delicious it made its way onto one of Baltimore's most prestigious country club menus and the cover of the cookbook! If you need instructions for how to ripen a mango and/or how to remove the flesh, visit the Product and Food Guide (see page 206). I use Valbreso French feta cheese because I like its zesty flavor and creamy texture. It's best to assemble the salad ingredients just prior to serving.

Prepare Celery Seed Dressing *(see page 137)*

4 cups shredded red cabbage
1 cup cubed ripe mango
1 ripe avocado, cut into bite-sized pieces
½ red pepper, cut into bite-sized pieces
2 scallions (green onions), thinly sliced
½ cup crumbled feta cheese
½ cup roasted, salted cashews
Salt and pepper, to taste

1. In a large bowl, gently toss the cabbage, mango, avocado, red pepper, and scallions.
2. Lightly coat the salad with dressing and toss to combine evenly.
3. Toss in feta cheese and cashews and season with salt and pepper. Serve immediately.

4 to 6 servings

Green Bean Salad with Gingered Walnuts, Cranberries, and Feta

This is a flavorful and colorful side dish that will be appreciated for its unusual combination of ingredients. I love to serve it with baked chicken. In this recipe I use Valbreso French feta cheese because I'm partial to its zesty flavor and creamy texture.

1 pound green beans, washed

DRESSING
1 teaspoon salt
Several grindings of freshly ground black pepper
1 teaspoon Dijon-style mustard
¼ cup apple cider vinegar
¾ cup extra virgin olive oil

GINGERED WALNUTS
1 tablespoon soy sauce or tamari
1 tablespoon dark rum
1 tablespoon toasted sesame oil
2 tablespoons packed brown sugar
¼ teaspoon ground ginger
½ cup walnut halves
Salt, to taste
½ cup dried cranberries
1 cup crumbled feta cheese

1. Fill a large pot with water and bring to a boil. Reduce heat slightly (water should be rumbling) and cook green beans, stirring occasionally for 7-10 minutes or until fork-tender. Immediately drain beans and transfer to a large bowl. When green beans are cool enough to handle, trim ends and cut into 1½-inch pieces.
2. In a 2-cup jar with a tight-fitting lid, combine salt, pepper, mustard, and vinegar. Shake until ingredients are well blended and salt has dissolved. Add olive oil and shake again to combine ingredients. Store at room temperature.
3. Preheat oven to 375°F.
4. In a medium bowl, whisk soy sauce or tamari, rum, sesame oil, brown sugar, and ginger until well combined. Add walnuts and toss to coat the nuts well. Place walnuts on a parchment-lined, rimmed baking sheet, and bake for 10 minutes. Using a slotted spoon,

transfer walnuts to a lightly oiled sheet of tin foil, disperse nuts in a single layer, and immediately season with salt.

5. In a large bowl, toss green beans with just enough dressing to coat the beans. Add cranberries, feta cheese, and walnuts to the beans and toss, adding more dressing if desired. Serve immediately.

4 servings

Bloody Mary Aspic

If you're planning a dinner party or family holiday gathering, this aspic is terrific with Marinated Beef Tenderloin, Creamy Chicken and Zucchini Casserole with Herb Stuffing or Creamy Seafood (see Index for recipes).

Aspics don't hold up well in hot weather; they melt just like ice cream! Regardless of the weather, aspics should not be unmolded until just before serving. Molds come in a variety of shapes and sizes and can be found in most kitchen-oriented stores. The ½-cup capacity individual aspic molds are festive for a seated dinner party or luncheon. If you're hosting a buffet party, use a 1-quart aspic mold. Aspic must be prepared a day in advance. The gelatin in the Jell-O needs at least 24 hours to properly gel.

> *3 cups tomato juice*
> *6 ounces lemon Jell-O gelatin*
> *2 tablespoons apple cider vinegar*
> *1 tablespoon prepared horseradish*
> *2 teaspoons Worcestershire sauce*

1. Generously oil a 1-quart aspic mold or eight ½-cup aspic molds with cooking spray.
2. In a medium saucepan over moderate heat, slowly bring tomato juice to a boil. When the tomato juice begins to bubble in spots, add Jell-O, vinegar, horseradish, and Worcestershire sauce. Remove from heat and stir for a few minutes until the sugar from the Jell-O has dissolved. Pour mixture into mold(s). If using individual ½-cup molds, fill each about ¾ full. Allow aspic to cool before covering and refrigerate overnight.
3. To remove aspic, fill a bowl larger than the diameter of the mold (the sink works well) with hot water. (Unmolding aspics can be tricky. The temperature of the water needs to be just right—too hot, the aspic will begin to melt; not hot enough, the aspic won't unmold.)
4. Set the mold in the water to a point just below the rim. Hold the mold there for a few seconds, wiggling it from side to side. When it begins to loosen from the sides of the mold, immediately remove from the water.
5. Place the serving plate or platter upside down over the mold. Hold the plate or platter and mold together with both hands and invert quickly. (If the first attempt doesn't work, refrigerate for about 5 minutes and go through the unmolding steps again.) Serve immediately.

10 to 12 servings

TOMATO RASPBERRY ASPIC

This is a sweet and savory aspic that pairs beautifully with beef, chicken (especially traditional chicken salad), and seafood. For an elegant dinner party, pair with Spinach-Stuffed Chicken Breasts (see Index for recipe).

1¼ cups water
9 ounces raspberry Jell-O gelatin
3 cans (15 ounces each) stewed tomatoes
6 drops Tabasco sauce or hot pepper sauce

1. Generously oil a 2-quart aspic mold with cooking spray.
2. In a medium saucepan, bring water to a boil, remove from heat, and stir in Jell-O. Stir mixture until the sugar has completely dissolved. Add tomatoes and Tabasco or hot pepper sauce and stir until evenly distributed. Pour mixture into aspic mold. Allow the aspic to cool before covering and refrigerate overnight.
3. To remove aspic, fill a bowl larger than the diameter of the mold (the sink works well) with hot but not boiling water. (Unmolding aspics can be tricky. The temperature of the water needs to be just right—too hot, the aspic will melt; not hot enough, the aspic won't unmold.)
4. Set the mold in the water to a point just below the rim. Hold the mold there for a few seconds, wiggling it from side to side. When it begins to loosen, immediately remove from the water.
5. Place the serving plate or platter upside down over the mold. Hold the plate or platter and mold together with both hands and invert quickly. (If the first attempt doesn't work, refrigerate for about 5 minutes and go through the unmolding steps again.) Serve immediately.

10 to 12 servings

ZUCCHINI SALAD
WITH WARM WALNUT DRESSING

Warm dressing barely wilts this prolific summer vegetable in a way that is so appealing. The key to its success is to serve it immediately after tossing it with the vegetables. Don't let it sit around, since the warm dressing will make the high water content of the zucchini even more watery.

2 medium zucchini, unpeeled and cut into thin julienne strips
1 cup thinly cut, julienned red pepper
2 medium shallots, thinly sliced
⅓ cup neutral oil
½ cup chopped walnuts
2 tablespoons seasoned rice vinegar
1 teaspoon sugar
Salt and pepper, to taste

1. In a large bowl, toss zucchini with red pepper and shallots.
2. Heat oil in a sauté pan over medium heat. Add walnuts and sauté for 3-5 minutes, stirring frequently (you may need to lower the temperature) to prevent the walnuts from burning.
3. Remove from heat and stir in vinegar (stand back, it will splatter). Add the sugar and season with salt and pepper. Pour mixture over zucchini/pepper/shallots and toss to coat evenly. Serve immediately.

4 servings

ICEBERG LETTUCE STUFFED WITH BLUE CHEESE DRESSING

Iceberg lettuce salads were a favorite when I was growing up, especially when my mother cut the head into wedges and spooned generous amounts of my uncle's popular blue cheese dressing all over the pale green leaves. Iceberg doesn't rank too high on the nutritional charts, but I love its crunchy texture. After all, the name iceberg (aka Crisphead) refers to the crisp, cold, clean characteristics of the leaves. To enhance its mild flavor, I created a flavorful, creamy blue cheese filling that gets stuffed into the center of the head. It's a fun recipe to prepare and one of the few lettuce leaf salads that is dressed and prepared in advance.

1 compact head of Iceberg lettuce
6 ounces light cream cheese, softened
⅓ cup blue cheese, crumbled
¼ cup mayonnaise
¼ cup finely chopped green pepper
¼ cup finely chopped red onion
¼ cup chopped chives
¼ cup finely chopped walnuts
1 teaspoon Worcestershire sauce
½ teaspoon salt
A few dashes Tabasco sauce or hot pepper sauce
Freshly ground black pepper, to taste
Croutons, if desired

1. To remove the center core from the head of lettuce, bang the head (core side down) against a hard surface. Gently pull out core. Wash the lettuce by running cold water into the center of the lettuce head for a few minutes. Invert the lettuce and allow any excess water to drain from lettuce for about 30 minutes. Refrigerate until ready to fill.

2. Hollow out center of lettuce (reserving lettuce for another salad) leaving a shell of about one inch.

3. In a medium bowl, beat cream cheese, blue cheese, and mayonnaise until smooth. Add green pepper, red onion, chives, walnuts, Worcestershire sauce, salt, and hot sauce. Mix until well blended. Spoon mixture into center of lettuce. Cover and refrigerate for several hours.

4. Cut iceberg into 6 wedges. Season with fresh ground pepper and croutons, if desired. Serve immediately.

6 servings

HEARTS OF PALM, MANGO, AND CASHEW SALAD WITH SALTY LIME DRESSING

The combination of sweet mango, crunchy cashews, and salty lime dressing makes an impressive and unusual lettuce salad.

⅓ cup olive oil
¼ cup fresh lime juice
1 teaspoon salt
6 very generous handfuls of red leaf lettuce, washed and torn into bite-sized pieces
1 ripe mango, cut into bite-sized pieces
1 can (14 ounces) sliced hearts of palm
½ cup roasted cashews

1. In a 1-cup jar with a tight-fitting lid, combine the olive oil, lime juice, and salt. Shake until well blended.
2. Place lettuce leaves in a large bowl and toss with enough dressing to coat the leaves. Divide lettuce among 6 serving plates.
3. In a small bowl, combine mango, hearts of palm, and cashews. Toss with enough dressing to coat the ingredients. Top lettuce leaves with mango mixture, distributing ingredients evenly. Serve immediately.

6 servings

flour power

INTRODUCING BREADS, BISCUITS, PIE CRUST AND FLAT CAKES

For me, one of the greatest culinary rewards is that of bread-making. It captures my senses in every way, and who can resist the aroma that wafts from the kitchen?

You will find an unusual and eclectic group of recipes in this chapter. There are two recipes for biscuits—one using sweet potatoes—two kinds of cornbread, a few breads with the addition of olives, some hearty breads using millet and flaxseed, a divine recipe for Muenster Cheese Bread, and a surprising loaf that includes butternut squash!

If you haven't tried bread-making, I encourage you to delve into this wonderful and appreciated culinary venture. Once you get the hang of it, I think you will be turning out loaves all the time. Try to keep in mind that making bread is not an exact science; as a rule, there is no right or wrong. I prefer to think of it as an art form, in which each loaf is a one-of-a-kind masterpiece. Here are some basic bread-making tips that should help you with the process.

Successful Bread-Making Tips

- It's best if all ingredients are at room temperature.
- Yeast should be fresh—check the expiration date before using. Yeast generally will not proof if the temperature of the liquid added is too cold or too hot. I use the inside of my wrist (an area that's sensitive to hot and cold) for testing the temperature of the liquid; it should be no hotter than what you would give a baby. Yeast requires a warm, damp environment to proof, as well as the addition of food (honey or sugar). Proofing yeast is like watching a chemistry experiment—ingredients reacting to other ingredients. The process takes 5-10 minutes, and the result should be a foamy and/or bubbly mixture.
- Dough can be quite temperamental and typically performs according to the weather conditions in your kitchen. Humidity makes for stickier dough, which means you'll need to add more flour while kneading. Colder/dryer conditions will require less flour during this process. When adding flour during the kneading process, measurements are not exact. Add flour until your dough is smooth and elastic. You will find many techniques for kneading dough; the perfect technique is the one that works best for you.
- Most bread dough requires at least two risings. During this process, dough should be in a warm environment, free of cold drafts. Suitable places might

include the top of a warm radiator, near something warming on the stove, or on a warm day, in natural sunlight. Rising times vary; on average, expect about one hour per rising.

- After a rising, you will always be asked to "punch down" the dough. Punching down is not so much about the act of punching as it is about the act of flattening. Using your fist or outstretched hand, push down the dough in order to deflate it.

BREADS
Flaxseed Bread 119
Kalamata Olive Bread 121
Muenster Cheese Bread 122
Butternut Squash Bread 123
Skillet Cornbread with Honey 124
Cream Cheese and Jam Bread 125
Moist and Rich Chili Corn Bread 126
Wheat Bread with Millet and Flax 127
Bread with Cream Cheese and Olive Filling 128

BISCUITS
Buttermilk Biscuits 130
Sweet Potato Biscuits 131

PIE CRUST AND FLAT CAKES
Homemade Pie Crust 132
Pan-Fried Flat Cakes with Scallions 133

FLAXSEED BREAD

This nutrient-rich, all-purpose loaf can be used to make sandwiches or served with soup. It also makes wonderful toast. It doesn't have grand rising properties, so don't expect it to double in bulk during either of the rising times. I purchase whole flaxseeds that I grind as needed.

1 cup boiling water
½ cup yellow corn flour
2 packages active dry yeast
1 tablespoon sugar
½ cup warm water
1 cup warm milk
2 teaspoons salt
¼ cup honey
½ cup raw wheat germ
½ cup whole flaxseeds, coarsely ground
3-4 cups unbleached all-purpose flour

1. Bring water to a boil in a medium pan over high heat. Add corn flour, decrease heat to low, and stir mixture vigorously. Cook the mixture until thick. Remove from heat and set aside.
2. In a large bowl, combine yeast, sugar, and warm water. Stir mixture until yeast dissolves. Proof for 5-15 minutes.
3. Add corn flour mixture to the yeast mixture and stir until well combined. Add the warm milk, salt, honey, wheat germ, and flaxseeds to the corn flour mixture and stir until incorporated.
4. Add flour 1 cup at a time, stirring well after each addition. When the dough begins to pull away from the sides of the bowl, turn out to a floured board and knead dough for about 10 minutes, adding more flour as necessary to keep the dough from sticking to the surface. Knead until dough is smooth and elastic.
5. Lightly coat a large bowl with oil. Transfer dough to the prepared bowl and coat all surfaces of the dough with the oil. Cover the bowl with a kitchen towel and allow the dough to rise for about 1 hour.
6. Punch dough down, cut in half and shape into 2 loaves.
7. Coat two 9 x 5 x 3-inch bread pans with cooking spray. Place the loaves in the prepared pans. Cover loaves with a kitchen towel and let the dough rise for about 1 hour.
8. Preheat oven to 425°F.
9. Bake loaves for 10 minutes. Decrease oven temperature to 350°F and bake an additional 20 minutes or until bread is light brown and sounds hollow when tapped on the top and bottom.

10. To crisp the crust, remove loaves from bread pans, place the loaves on the oven rack, and bake for 1-2 minutes.

11. Place loaves on wire rack to cool before slicing.

2 loaves

KALAMATA OLIVE BREAD

This fabulous loaf of bread has a pronounced Kalamata flavor, and it is one you will be proud to share. I use good-quality Kalamata olives that have not been previously pitted. It takes a few minutes to remove the pit from the olive, but I find they taste so much better than the pitted version. This is in keeping with my philosophy that all food tastes better when it's just been cut, sliced, shredded or, in this case, pitted!

1 package active dry yeast
½ teaspoon sugar
1 cup warm water
2 tablespoons neutral oil
1 teaspoons salt
1 cup pitted and finely chopped Kalamata olives
2-2½ cups unbleached all-purpose flour

1. In a large bowl, combine yeast, sugar, and ¼ cup of warm water. Stir mixture until yeast dissolves. Proof for about 5 minutes.
2. Add remaining water, oil, salt, and olives. Add 1 cup flour and mix well. Add more flour and when dough begins to pull away from the sides of the bowl, turn the dough out to a floured surface and knead, adding more flour to keep it from sticking to the surface. Knead the dough for 8-10 minutes, until it is smooth and elastic.
3. Lightly coat a large bowl with oil. Transfer the dough to the prepared bowl and lightly coat all surfaces of the dough with the oil. Cover the bowl with a kitchen towel and allow the dough to rise for about 1½ hours.
4. Punch dough down and shape into a loaf.
5. Generously coat a 9 x 5 x 3-inch bread pan with cooking spray. Place the loaf in the prepared pan. Cover the loaf with a kitchen towel and let it rise for another 1½ hours.
6. Preheat oven to 350°F.
7. Bake loaf for 40-45 minutes or until it sounds hollow when tapped on the top and bottom. Allow loaf to cool completely before cutting.

1 loaf

MUENSTER CHEESE BREAD

The first time I prepared this bread was on a cold and blistery winter day. We ate this divine loaf, hot from the oven, with steaming bowls of Beef and Broccoli Soup (see Index for the recipe) in front of a roaring fire.

2 packages active dry yeast
1 teaspoons sugar
1 cup warm water
¼ cup neutral oil
2 teaspoons salt
2-3 cups unbleached all-purpose flour
4 cups shredded (1 pound) Muenster cheese

1. In a large bowl, combine yeast, sugar, and warm water. Stir mixture until yeast dissolves. Proof for about 5 minutes.
2. Add oil, salt, and 2 cups of flour. Stir until well combined, adding enough of the remaining flour to make a soft dough.
3. Turn out to a floured surface and knead dough (adding more flour as needed) for 6-8 minutes or until you have a smooth, elastic dough.
4. Lightly coat a large bowl with cooking spray. Transfer the dough to the prepared bowl and coat all surfaces of the dough with the oil. Cover with a kitchen towel and allow the dough to rise for about 1 hour.
5. Punch dough down and roll into a 16-inch diameter.
6. Coat a 9-inch round pan with cooking spray.
7. Carefully transfer dough to the prepared pan and allow the dough to drape over the sides of the pan. Top the center of the dough with the shredded cheese.
8. Lift the overlapping dough from the sides of the pan and drop the dough over the cheese as though you were creating pleats. Carefully turn loaf over so pleats are facing the bottom of the pan. Cover with a kitchen towel and let rise for about 30 minutes.
9. Preheat oven to 375°F.
10. Bake loaf for 45 minutes.
11. Let stand for 10 minutes before slicing.

1 loaf

BUTTERNUT SQUASH BREAD

This recipe was the result of some leftover butternut squash. It's a lovely loaf with a beautiful buttery color. The flavor is like butternut squash itself—mellow. Slather warm slices with butter or toast it. You can also use it for sandwiches or serve with steaming bowls of soup.

> *2 packages active dry yeast*
> *1 teaspoon sugar*
> *½ cup warm water*
> *1¼ cups cooked butternut squash, mashed*
> *1 cup warm milk*
> *2 tablespoons neutral oil*
> *1¼ cups brown sugar*
> *3 teaspoons salt*
> *1 cup wheat germ*
> *5-6 cups unbleached all-purpose flour*

1. In a large bowl, combine yeast, sugar, and warm water. Stir mixture until yeast dissolves. Proof yeast for 5-15 minutes.
2. Add the squash, milk, oil, brown sugar, salt, and wheat germ to the yeast mixture. Add flour 1 cup at a time. When the dough begins to pull away from the sides of the bowl, turn out to a floured board and knead the dough for about 10 minutes, adding more flour as necessary to keep the dough from sticking to the surface. Knead until dough is smooth and elastic, about 10 minutes.
3. Lightly coat a large bowl with oil. Transfer the dough to the prepared bowl and coat all surfaces of the dough with the oil. Cover the bowl with a kitchen towel and allow the dough to rise for about 1 hour.
4. Punch dough down and divide into 2 loaves.
5. Coat two 9 x 5 x 3-inch bread pans with cooking spray. Place each loaf in the prepared pan. Cover the loaves with a kitchen towel and let them rise until doubled in bulk, about 30 minutes.
6. Preheat oven to 375°F.
7. Bake loaves for 25-30 minutes or until golden brown.
8. Remove loaves from pans and allow them to cool on a wire rack for about 10 minutes before slicing.

2 loaves

SKILLET CORNBREAD WITH HONEY

This rustic-looking cornbread recipe is easy to prepare and complements so many dishes.

1 cup unbleached all-purpose flour
¾ cup yellow corn flour
3 tablespoons sugar
5 teaspoons baking powder
1 teaspoon salt
2 eggs
1¼ cups buttermilk
2 tablespoons neutral oil
Honey and butter

1. Preheat oven to 350°F.
2. Generously oil a 10-inch cast iron skillet with cooking oil.
3. In a large bowl, combine the all-purpose flour, corn flour, sugar, baking powder, and salt.
4. In a large bowl, whisk the eggs with the buttermilk and oil.
5. Make a well in the center of the dry ingredients. Add the egg mixture and stir just to combine.
6. Transfer batter to cast iron skillet and bake for 10-12 minutes or until a toothpick inserted into the center comes out clean. Remove skillet from oven.
7. Move oven rack to the top rung and switch oven temperature to broil. Brown the top of the cornbread for 1-2 minutes. Watch carefully—there is a narrow window between a brown top and a scorched one.
8. Using chopsticks or a fork, prick the cornbread in several places. Drizzle desired amount of honey over cornbread. Serve immediately with butter.

6 to 8 servings

CREAM CHEESE AND JAM BREAD

This is lovely to serve with afternoon tea, and it's also impressive brunch fare. It received high approval ratings when I served it with scrambled eggs, sausage, and bacon.

1 package active dry yeast
1 teaspoon honey
⅔ cup warm water
½ teaspoon salt
1¼ cups unbleached all-purpose flour
4 ounces cream cheese, softened
¼ cup of your favorite jam or preserves

1. In a large bowl, combine the yeast and honey with ⅓ cup of water. Allow the yeast to proof for about 5 minutes.
2. Add remaining water, salt, and 1 cup of flour, then stir to combine ingredients. Transfer the dough to a floured surface and knead until dough is smooth and elastic, adding more flour as needed to keep the dough from sticking to the surface.
3. Lightly coat a medium bowl with cooking spray. Transfer the dough to the bowl and lightly coat all surfaces of the dough with the oil. Cover and set in a warm, draft-free place and let rise for about 30 minutes.
4. Lightly coat a work surface with flour. Punch down dough and roll into an 11 x 7-inch rectangle. Spread cheese along the center of the rectangle. Top the cheese with jam or preserves. Roll the rectangle into the shape of a log. Pinch each end to seal and tuck ends under. With a sharp knife, make several slits across the top of the log. Carefully transfer loaf to a parchment-lined rimmed baking sheet. Cover with a kitchen towel and let rise for about 1 hour.
5. Preheat oven to 375°F.
6. Bake for 30 minutes or until golden brown. Let stand for 10 minutes before slicing.

1 loaf

MOIST AND RICH CHILI CORNBREAD

This is a moist and rich bread with bold flavors, hence its name. I serve it often because it complements a variety of dishes—Mexican fare, soups, salads, and casseroles—and it always receives high approval ratings. I often serve this with Seafood Lasagna with Fire-Roasted Tomatoes and Brandied Carrots with Peas (see Index for recipes) when I'm hosting an elegant dinner party. It's such a complementary trio. I like to prepare this during the summer months when fresh corn is plentiful. (Frozen corn may be substituted.) I chop half the amount of corn because it's a great contrast with the whole corn kernels.

¾ cup yellow corn flour
¼ cup unbleached all-purpose flour
2 teaspoons salt
3 teaspoons baking powder
2 eggs
¼ cup milk
¾ cup sour cream
⅓ cup olive oil
1 can (4 ounces) chopped green chilies
¾ cup corn kernels
¾ cup chopped corn kernels
1 cup shredded Monterey Jack cheese

1. Preheat oven to 350°F.
2. In a medium bowl, combine corn flour, all-purpose flour, salt, and baking powder.
3. In a large bowl, whisk the eggs with the milk. Add the sour cream, olive oil, and green chilies. Stir until fully combined. Add corn kernels and chopped corn kernels to the egg mixture and mix until fully incorporated. Add flour mixture to wet ingredients and stir to combine.
4. Transfer batter into a generously oiled 11 x 7-inch (2-liter) baking dish.
5. Bake for 1 hour. Serve immediately.

8 servings

WHEAT BREAD
WITH MILLET AND FLAX

I am a fan of millet for many reasons. It is highly nutritious, non-glutinous, and, like buckwheat and quinoa, it's easy to digest. Millet is tasty, with a mildly sweet, nut-like flavor, and contains a myriad of beneficial nutrients. It is nearly fifteen percent protein, contains mega amounts of fiber, and is high in vitamins and minerals. I lightly toast the millet seeds in this bread recipe because it enhances their flavor.

1 package active dry yeast
1 teaspoon sugar
1¾ cup warm water
½ cup millet seeds, toasted
2 tablespoons molasses
2 teaspoons salt
2 tablespoons neutral oil
½ cup whole flaxseeds, coarsely ground
4-4½ cups whole wheat flour

1. Preheat toaster oven or oven to 350°F.
2. In a large bowl, combine yeast, sugar, and ½ cup of warm water. Stir mixture until yeast dissolves. Proof for about 5 minutes.
3. Place millet seeds on a rimmed baking sheet and toast until lightly browned. (Watch closely; there's a narrow window between toasted and burned.)
4. Add remaining water, molasses, salt, oil, millet, and flaxseeds to the yeast mixture, then stir until well combined. Add 2 cups of flour and mix well. Continue to stir, adding a little flour at a time. When dough begins to pull away from the sides of the bowl, turn out to a floured surface. Knead the dough for 5-7 minutes or until dough becomes smooth and elastic.
5. Shape the dough into a loaf and place in an oiled 9 x 5 x 3-inch bread pan.
6. Cover bread with a kitchen towel and allow it to rise in a warm, draft-free spot until doubled in bulk, about 1 hour.
7. Preheat oven to 350°F.
8. Bake bread for 45-50 minutes or until loaf sounds hollow when tapped on the top and bottom. Allow bread to cool slightly before slicing.

1 loaf

BREAD WITH CREAM CHEESE AND OLIVE FILLING

This stuffed bread is as delicious to eat as it is easy to make. It's the kind of recipe your taste testers will think you have labored over all day.

BREAD DOUGH
1 package active dry yeast
1 teaspoon sugar
1 cup warm water
1½-2 cups unbleached all-purpose flour
¼ cup wheat germ
1 teaspoon salt

CREAM CHEESE AND OLIVE FILLING
½ cup whipped cream cheese
½ teaspoon oregano
½ teaspoon thyme
½ teaspoon tarragon
½ teaspoon basil
A few grindings of fresh black pepper
¾ cup pitted Kalamata olives, finely chopped

1. To prepare the dough, combine yeast, sugar, and warm water in a medium bowl. Stir the mixture until the yeast dissolves. Proof yeast for 5-15 minutes.
2. In a large bowl, combine flour, wheat germ, and salt. Add yeast mixture and stir until well blended. Turn dough out onto a lightly floured surface. Knead dough until bread is smooth and elastic, adding flour as needed to keep the dough from sticking to the surface. Knead for about 5 minutes.
3. Lightly coat a large bowl with cooking spray. Transfer dough to the prepared bowl and coat all surfaces of the dough with the oil. Cover with a kitchen towel and allow the dough to rise for about 1 hour.
4. While the dough is rising, prepare the filling. In a medium bowl, combine cream cheese with oregano, thyme, tarragon, basil, and black pepper. Cover and set aside.
5. Lightly coat a work surface with flour. Punch down dough and roll into an 11 x 7-inch rectangle.
6. Spread cheese mixture evenly over rectangle, leaving a 1-inch border. Top cheese with black olives, gently pressing them into the cheese mixture.

7. Roll the rectangle into the shape of a log. Pinch each end to seal and tuck ends under. With a sharp knife, make several slits across the top of the log. Carefully transfer the loaf to a parchment-lined, rimmed baking sheet. Cover with a kitchen towel and let rise for about 1 hour.

8. Preheat oven to 375°F.

9. Bake loaf for 30 minutes or until golden brown.

10. Let stand for 10 minutes before slicing. Serve immediately.

1 loaf

BUTTERMILK BISCUITS

Since this recipe doesn't call for butter, you can justify flooding the biscuits with butter hot from the oven! We like to sweeten them (like Southerners do) with honey. Biscuit dough is best if minimally handled. Over-stirring, over-kneading, and/or over-rolling can turn what is meant to be a fluffy biscuit into a dense and heavy biscuit.

1 package active dry yeast
1 teaspoon sugar
½ cup warm water
3 cups unbleached all-purpose flour
2 cups cake flour
¼ cup sugar
1 teaspoon baking powder
1 teaspoon baking soda
1 teaspoon salt
½ cup neutral oil
2 cups buttermilk
Butter and honey

1. In a medium bowl, combine yeast, 1 teaspoon sugar, and warm water. Stir until mixture is dissolved. Proof for about 5 minutes.
2. In a large mixing bowl, combine all-purpose flour, cake flour, ¼ cup sugar, baking powder, baking soda, and salt. Slowly drizzle oil over flour mixture and toss with a fork until mixture resembles coarse meal. Add yeast mixture and buttermilk to flour mixture and stir until just combined. Cover and refrigerate overnight.
3. Preheat oven to 450°F.
4. Heavily cover a work surface with flour. Turn out dough and knead a few times. Roll until dough is about 1 inch thick. Cut with a 3-inch biscuit cutter. Arrange biscuits on 2 parchment-lined baking sheets.
5. Bake biscuits for 11-13 minutes or until golden. Serve immediately and pass the butter and honey to your guests.

24 biscuits

SWEET POTATO BISCUITS

Rather than cutting the dough with a biscuit cutter, I cut these into squares. I love their informal, rustic appearance. Slather hot biscuits with butter and honey, or fill them with slices of Baked Ham (see page 81). Sweet potatoes' water content (all vegetables for that matter) varies greatly. You may need to add more flour to achieve a workable dough. Try to avoid over-stirring, over-kneading, and/or over-rolling. Doing so can turn what is meant to be a fluffy biscuit into a dense and heavy biscuit.

> *2 cups unbleached all-purpose flour*
> *⅓ cup yellow corn flour*
> *1½ teaspoons baking powder*
> *½ teaspoon salt*
> *⅓ cup neutral oil*
> *1 cup cooked mashed sweet potato*
> *½ cup buttermilk*
> *2 tablespoons honey*
> *Butter*

1. Preheat oven to 400°F.
2. In a large bowl, combine all-purpose flour, corn flour, baking powder, and salt. Drizzle oil over flour mixture. Toss flour with a fork, allowing the flour to absorb the oil. Add sweet potato, buttermilk, and honey. Knead dough a few times (dough will be very sticky) until well combined. If the mixture seems too wet, add more all-purpose flour.
3. Cover a work surface with flour. Turn dough onto floured surface and roll into a rough 9-inch square. Cut into 16 squares.
4. Transfer squares to a parchment-lined or generously oiled, rimmed baking sheet and bake for 15-20 minutes or until golden brown. Serve immediately and pass the butter to your guests.

16 biscuits

HOMEMADE PIE CRUST

Contrary to what others might say, I think making homemade pie crust is rather simple. Once you see how easy it is, you may never go back to store-bought. Perfection has no place here; homemade is supposed to look homemade. Surprisingly, oil replaces the shortening usually found in pie crust recipes, making this crust a heart-healthier alternative. (Use shortening if you prefer.) The weather often affects how dough comes together. Add more water (a little at a time) if dough doesn't come together or seems dry. Dough can be prepared in advance and refrigerated until ready to use. For best results, allow the dough to come to room temperature before rolling.

> 1⅛ cup unbleached all-purpose flour
> ½ teaspoon salt
> ¼ cup neutral oil or vegetable shortening
> 2½ tablespoons cold water, or more, to form a soft dough

1. In a large bowl, combine the flour and salt. Add oil or shortening to flour mixture and toss with your fingers until mixture is coarse. Slowly add cold water. Using your hands, bring flour mixture together until ingredients are fully incorporated. Knead a few times.
2. Let the dough rest for about 5 minutes.
3. Preheat oven to 425°F.
4. Lightly flour a work surface. Begin to roll the dough and when it resists, let it rest for several minutes. Continue rolling the dough and when it begins to resist again, let it rest.
5. Roll dough into a 12-inch round.
6. Transfer dough to a 9-inch pie plate and flute edges using the dough that overlaps the pie plate. Prick the shell in several places with a fork.
7. Bake for 12-15 minutes or until light brown.

1 (9-inch) pie crust

PAN-FRIED FLAT CAKES
WITH SCALLIONS

These are fun to eat if you have a counter service-style kitchen so guests can eat the flat cakes hot from the skillet. You can also make them in batches and keep them in a warm oven until serving. Don't worry about equal portions when dividing the dough or creating the perfect circle when rolling the flat cakes; perfection doesn't have a place here. These savory flat cakes are delicious when dipped into Sesame Ginger Dressing (see page 139).

1 cup unbleached all-purpose flour
⅓ cup brown rice flour
½ cup scallions (green onions), thinly sliced (green part only)
½ teaspoon salt
½ cup water
Neutral oil for skillet

1. In a medium bowl, combine all-purpose flour, brown rice flour, scallions, and salt. Add water and stir to combine. Knead dough for a few minutes, adding more flour if necessary to keep dough from sticking to the bowl.
2. Divide dough into 6 pieces.
3. Lightly coat a work surface with flour. Roll each piece into a thin circle, about 8 inches in diameter.
4. Cover the bottom of a large skillet with oil. Over medium high heat, cook flat cakes for 1-2 minutes, in batches, until brown on each side.
5. Transfer to a platter and cut into wedges. Serve immediately with Sesame Ginger Dressing.

6 flat cakes

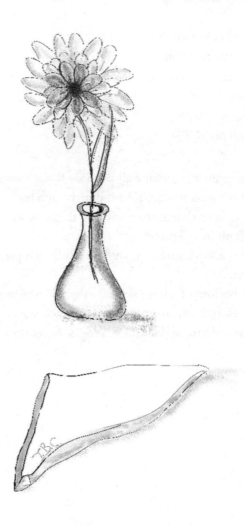

complementers

INTRODUCING SALAD DRESSINGS, SAUCES, AND MISCELLANEOUS

I grew up eating salads with homemade dressings. Anything with a sauce my mother made from scratch. I appreciated her efforts to prepare condiments from scratch (everything we ate for that matter) using wholesome ingredients. She was devoted to feeding her brood of five food that was prepared without additives or chemicals. Store-bought and convenient was just coming into vogue when I was a child, but seldom did this convenience ever wind up in her grocery cart. The food industry has come a long way since then. Now we can purchase healthier, store-bought dressings, sauces, spreads, and pie crusts. In my opinion, however, nothing compares with the taste of homemade, and besides, it evokes wonderful memories of the delicious meals my mother so lovingly prepared from scratch.

CELERY SEED DRESSING

This crowd-pleasing dressing is delicious tossed with any combination of salad ingredients. It will turn an ordinary pasta side dish into a tasty pasta salad. This dressing will last for several days in the refrigerator.

⅓ cup sugar
1 teaspoon salt
1 teaspoon dry mustard
1 teaspoon freshly minced onion
¼ cup apple cider vinegar
1 cup canola or neutral oil
1 teaspoon celery seeds

1. In a medium bowl, combine sugar, salt, and dry mustard. Add onion and apple cider vinegar, then whisk until sugar has dissolved.
2. Slowly add oil and whisk until dressing thickens. Add celery seeds and whisk until well blended.
3. Transfer to a 2-cup jar with a tight-fitting lid and serve immediately, or refrigerate until serving time. Allow the dressing to come to room temperature before using. Shake well prior to using.

About 1½ cups

SESAME DIJON DRESSING

This super-simple dressing is abundant with flavor and complements the ordinary and often bland cold pasta salad. It is also a delicious spread for steak, chicken, or vegetable sandwiches.

½ cup mayonnaise
1 tablespoon seasoned rice vinegar
1 tablespoon soy sauce or tamari
1 tablespoon Dijon-style mustard
1 tablespoon toasted sesame oil

1. In a medium bowl, combine mayonnaise, vinegar, soy sauce, mustard, and sesame oil. Whisk until smooth. Cover and refrigerate until ready to use.

About ⅔ cup

SESAME GINGER DRESSING

Here's a versatile dressing that can be used to toss with any combination of vegetables, shrimp, or pasta. I especially love it tossed with soba noodles. It's also a delicious dipping sauce for Pan-Fried Flat Cakes with Scallions (see page 133).

> ¼ cup fresh gingerroot, peeled
> ⅓ cup neutral oil
> 3 tablespoons honey
> 3 tablespoons tamari or soy sauce
> 2 tablespoons seasoned rice vinegar
> 1 tablespoon toasted sesame oil
> Salt and pepper, to taste
> 2 tablespoons toasted sesame seeds

1. In a blender or food processor, combine gingerroot, oil, honey, tamari, vinegar, and sesame oil. Blend until smooth. Season with salt and pepper and add sesame seeds.
2. Transfer to a 2-cup jar with a tight-fitting lid. Shake well and serve immediately, or cover and refrigerate until serving. Allow the dressing to come to room temperature before using.

About 1 cup

SWEET AND SOUR SALAD DRESSING

This is a simple, tasty dressing that complements any assortment of lettuce leaves, shredded cabbage, vegetables, cooked shrimp, or pasta. Grate the onion using a Microplane box grater or hand-held grater. This dressing is best made a day in advance to allow the flavors to mingle.

½ cup neutral oil
⅓ cup sugar
¼ cup apple cider vinegar
2 tablespoons ketchup
2 tablespoons grated onion
½ teaspoon celery seed
½ teaspoon dry mustard
1 teaspoon salt
¼ teaspoon paprika

1. Place all ingredients in a medium bowl. Whisk until sugar dissolves and mixture is fully incorporated.
2. Transfer to a 2-cup jar with a tight-fitting lid and refrigerate overnight. Allow the dressing to come to room temperature before serving. Shake well prior to using.

About 1 cup

Apple Barbecue Sauce

This is a zesty flavor-booster for spare ribs, beef, chicken, shrimp, and tofu.

> *1 can (8 ounces) tomato sauce*
> *½ cup apple jelly*
> *¼ cup apple cider vinegar*
> *2 tablespoons packed brown sugar*
> *2 tablespoons water*
> *1 teaspoon Tabasco sauce or hot pepper sauce*
> *¼ teaspoon salt*

1. In a medium saucepan, combine tomato sauce, apple jelly, vinegar, brown sugar, water, Tabasco or hot pepper sauce, and salt. Stir until well blended.
2. Bring mixture to a gentle boil. Reduce heat and simmer, stirring occasionally for about 15 minutes.

About 1⅓ cups

MAPLE CRANBERRY SAUCE WITH WALNUTS

I was about six years old when I remember my first experience with cranberry sauce. My grandmother was preparing our family Christmas dinner: turkey, gravy, stuffing, green bean casserole, the best creamed corn, mashed potatoes, and the brightest colored food served: ½-inch-thick disks of jellied cranberry sauce.

I watched as my grandmother carefully opened both ends of the cranberry can. With a few shakes, a garnet-colored, shimmering, jelly-like tubular form popped out, making a swishing sound on its way to the platter. I recall with clarity the perfectly circular indentations that marked the cylinder. My grandmother told me that when the can is filled with the cranberry mixture, the mixture gels, and the can molds the mixture.

It's been years since I bought a can of cranberry sauce, opting instead to buy fresh berries and make my own, which comes out nothing like the jellied version from my youth. Homemade cranberry sauce requires minimal preparation. In fact, the ingredients can be assembled in probably the same amount of time it took my grandmother to prepare and platter the canned version.

These berries get the added benefit of flavors that come from naturally sweetened maple syrup, cranberry-raspberry juice, and orange zest. The result is yummy and a great complement to Thanksgiving and Christmas dinner, but don't limit this delicious sauce to the holidays. It's a terrific spread for chicken and/or turkey sandwiches, and it's beautiful spooned over vanilla or coconut ice cream. You can successfully prepare this simple sauce in advance, and it will last for several days in the refrigerator.

12 ounces fresh cranberries, rinsed
1 cup pure maple syrup
1 cup cranberry-raspberry juice
Grated zest of one orange
1 cup chopped walnuts

1. In a large saucepan, combine cranberries, maple syrup, juice, and orange zest. Bring mixture to a boil. Decrease heat and cook for 5-10 minutes, stirring occasionally until cranberries pop open.
2. When the sauce has cooled, stir in walnuts.
3. Transfer the sauce to a container, cover, and refrigerate until serving time.

2½-3 cups

CAPONATA

Caponata is a sweet and sour Sicilian adaptation of ratatouille, the classic stewed vegetable dish that comes from the French region of Provence. The versatile flavors in Caponata intensify with age, so it's best to prepare a day or two in advance. This flavorful dish is a tasty and unique accompaniment to poached or scrambled eggs and steak sandwiches. Include it in your next grilled cheese sandwich for a really memorable taste treat.

1 medium eggplant, unpeeled, cut into ½-inch slices
Olive oil
2 tablespoons olive oil
1 cup finely chopped celery
½ cup finely chopped onion
2 cloves garlic, minced
1 cup chopped fresh tomato
3 tablespoons tomato sauce
2 tablespoons seasoned rice vinegar
½ cup pitted and chopped Kalamata olives
2 tablespoons small capers
1 teaspoon sugar
½ teaspoon salt or to taste
Several grindings of fresh black pepper
2 tablespoons chopped fresh parsley

1. Preheat oven to 500°F.
2. Arrange eggplant on a rimmed baking sheet. Brush both sides of eggplant with olive oil. Bake for 15 minutes, turning eggplant slices halfway through cooking time. When eggplant is cool enough to handle, cut into small chunks.
3. In a sauté pan over medium heat, heat olive oil and add celery, onion, and garlic, then sauté for about 5 minutes, stirring frequently. Add chopped tomato, tomato sauce, vinegar, olives, capers, sugar, salt and pepper. Reduce heat to low and cook for an additional 10 minutes. Remove from heat and stir in eggplant and parsley.
4. Allow the Caponata to cool before covering and refrigerate overnight. Serve Caponata at room temperature.

Serves a crowd

BETTER BUTTER

When you combine equal amounts of butter and oil, you get nearly the entire flavor of butter with only half the saturated fat and cholesterol. If you prefer a savory, robust-tasting butter, use olive oil in this recipe; for an all-purpose flavor, combine butter with a neutral oil. Keep unused portions of Better Butter refrigerated.

8 tablespoons (1 stick) butter, softened
½ cup olive or neutral oil

1. In a medium bowl, blend butter and oil with a wire whisk or use a stand mixer. Blend until fully incorporated.
2. Transfer mixture to a container and refrigerate for several hours (or until firm) before serving.

About 1 cup

SUMMER PESTO

I prepare Summer Pesto throughout the summer when basil is plentiful. It's delicious tossed with warm pasta, and I often stack slices of colorful summer tomatoes (green zebra, orange, and red) with slices of mozzarella cheese that I've slathered with pesto. It's also called for in the Pesto Cheese Torte recipe (see page 29).

2½ cups firmly packed fresh basil leaves
2 large garlic cloves
½ cup chopped almonds
½ cup freshly grated Parmesan cheese
½ cup olive oil
Salt, to taste

1. In a food processor fitted with a steel blade, combine basil leaves, garlic cloves, chopped almonds, and Parmesan cheese. Pulse a few times.
2. While the motor is running, drizzle olive oil through the feed tube and whirl the mixture until well combined. Season with salt to taste. Transfer pesto to a container and serve immediately or refrigerate until serving.

About 1 cup

SWEET WHIPPED CREAM

It's always a surprise to learn that people think it's difficult to prepare whipped cream. To the contrary, it's very simple. Homemade whipped cream is so much more flavorful than store-bought, and besides, it doesn't have added chemical stabilizers to keep it in whipped form. For cream to properly whip, place the bowl and/or the beaters in the freezer for several hours prior to preparing the whipped cream.

>*1 cup heavy whipping cream*
>*1 teaspoon vanilla*
>*2 tablespoons confectioners' sugar*

1. Place whipping cream in the bowl of a stand mixer and beat on medium high-speed.
2. When the cream begins to thicken, increase speed slightly and beat until soft peaks form. (Be careful not to over-whip the cream or it will turn to butter.)
3. Fold in vanilla and confectioner's sugar. Serve immediately or refrigerate until serving.

About 2 cups

MARINATED SWEET ONIONS

These sweet onions are delicious with vegan burgers, grilled hamburgers, hot dogs, spare ribs, sausage and steak.

¼ cup apple cider vinegar
¼ cup water
¼ cup sugar
2 medium sweet onions, thinly sliced (Vidalia, etc.)
¼ cup mayonnaise
¼ teaspoon celery seeds

1. In a large bowl, combine vinegar, water, and sugar. Allow sugar to dissolve for about 15 minutes. Add onions and toss with vinegar mixture. Cover and let stand at room temperature for about 8 hours or overnight.
2. Drain onions, discarding marinade.
3. In a small bowl, combine mayonnaise and celery seeds. Toss mixture with onions. Serve immediately or cover and refrigerate until serving.

4 servings

HONEY-GLAZED PINEAPPLE

This is as tasty as it is beautiful. When the piping hot, honey-glazed pineapple gets doused with brown sugar and Grand Marnier, and you set fire to the mixture, it billows into a flame! If the flame part is of concern, it only lasts a few seconds and is worth it for the dramatic presentation. (I recommend using long matches or a hand-held lighter.) This pineapple dish is a complementary accompaniment to baked ham, and it is also delicious spooned over coconut ice cream or frozen yogurt.

¼ cup honey
1 tablespoon curry powder
1 tablespoon vanilla extract
1 pineapple, peeled, cored, and cut into bite-sized pieces
¼ cup packed brown sugar
¼ cup Grand Marnier liqueur

1. Preheat oven to 500°F.
2. In a large bowl, combine honey, curry powder, and vanilla. Add pineapple and toss to coat ingredients well.
3. Transfer pineapple mixture to a rimmed baking sheet and cook for 10 minutes.
4. Remove and sprinkle brown sugar evenly over the pineapple. Pour Grand Marnier over pineapple. Light a hand-held lighter or a long match, stand back, and ignite the mixture. Serve immediately.

4 to 6 servings

CITRUS AND PEACH MARMALADE

When I was a toddler, every summer I watched as my mother, grandmothers, and aunts passionately preserved the harvest's bounty. This was important work because what they canned would sustain their families through the winter months. (Canning involves proper vessel temperatures; if you don't know anything about preserving food, *www.freshpreserving.com* offers a comprehensive, easy-to-follow preserving guide.) Come early spring, the place where this marmalade once crowded my grandmother's pantry was empty.

2 oranges, unpeeled and quartered
½ lemon, unpeeled
6 medium peaches, peeled and chopped
3½ cups sugar

1. Place oranges and lemon in food processor and pulse until mixture is well chopped. Transfer orange/lemon mixture to a large bowl, add peaches and sugar. Mix until well combined. Cover and refrigerate overnight.
2. Transfer orange/lemon mixture to a large saucepan and allow mixture to come to room temperature. Over moderate heat, bring mixture to a slow boil and boil for 20 minutes, stirring frequently.
3. Carefully pour into sterilized jars and seal immediately.

About 5 (8-ounce) jars

Oatmeal Croutons with Honey and Garlic

I love anything crunchy tossed into lettuce leaf salads. Some of my favorite crunchy additions are nuts, bread croutons, toasted sesame seeds, and especially these savory and sweet oatmeal croutons. It's a simple and surprising combination of ingredients that seem unusual to add to a tossed green salad, but taste-testers have never been disappointed. Any leftover croutons will keep for several days if stored in an airtight container.

1 cup quick-cooking oatmeal
¼ cup neutral oil
¼ cup honey
⅛ cup minced garlic (about 3 large cloves)
Salt, to taste

1. Preheat oven to 350°F.
2. In a medium bowl, combine oatmeal with oil, honey, and garlic. Stir until the ingredients are well distributed.
3. Transfer mixture to a parchment-lined baking sheet and bake for 10 minutes. Using a metal spatula, turn oats and bake an additional 10-15 minutes or until chestnut brown. Remove from oven, turn again, and season with salt.
4. Allow oatmeal croutons to cool completely on baking sheet until crisp. Serve immediately or transfer to an airtight container.

About 1 cup

morning glories

INTRODUCING MUFFINS, PANCAKES, COFFEE CAKE AND EGG DISHES

This eclectic bunch includes some familiar breakfast recipes and some that have a unique twist, like Parsnip Pancakes with Ginger Preserves and one of my all-time favorites, Poached Eggs over Buttery Shredded Wheat. There are some fun and impressive recipes like the Popover Pancake—this emerges from the oven puffed up like a ball!

MUFFINS, PANCAKES, AND COFFEE CAKE

EGG DISHES

BRAN MUFFINS

The first time I made these for my teen-aged nephew, he ate the whole batch in one sitting!

3 tablespoons neutral oil
2 tablespoons honey
2 tablespoons molasses
1 egg
1½ cups milk
1 cup whole wheat flour
1½ cups bran
½ teaspoon salt
1 teaspoon baking soda
½ cup flaxseeds, ground

1. Preheat oven to 375°F.
2. Generously oil 8 compartments of a 12-capacity muffin pan with cooking spray.
3. In a large bowl, whisk together oil, honey, molasses, egg, and milk. Mix until well blended.
4. In a medium bowl, combine whole wheat flour, bran, salt, baking soda, and flaxseeds. Add flour mixture to liquid mixture and combine until ingredients are incorporated. Spoon muffin batter into prepared muffin compartments, filling them just to the top.
5. Bake for 17-20 minutes or until a toothpick inserted in the center of a muffin comes out clean. Let muffins rest for about 5 minutes before serving.

8 large muffins

Popover Pancake

This pancake cooks in a cast iron skillet in a very hot oven (similar to the traditional English popovers that also bake in a very hot oven) and puffs up stunningly, albeit briefly. Then, just moments out of the oven, it deflates. But the result is a crispy pancake with a custardy interior. It's impressive and delicious, but to pull it off, you have to bake it in a cast iron skillet and you must use skim milk (reduced fat translates to more crispiness). This, and the cornstarch (also known for its crisping ability), is precisely what makes the Popover Pancake crispy. Serve with fresh fruit and cottage cheese, or with pork or vegetarian sausage, or bacon.

It's important that the skillet is at just the right temperature. If you don't think you can prepare the Popover Pancake batter in 10 minutes (the time it takes for the cast iron skillet to get hot), prepare the batter first, then place the skillet in the oven.

> *2 tablespoons neutral oil*
> *1 cup unbleached all-purpose flour*
> *¼ cup cornstarch*
> *1 teaspoon salt*
> *3 eggs, at room temperature*
> *1¼ cup skim milk*
> *1 teaspoon vanilla*
> *Butter and syrup*

1. Preheat oven to 450°F.
2. Place oil in a 10-inch cast iron skillet. Heat skillet in oven for 10 minutes.
3. In a large bowl, combine flour, cornstarch, and salt.
4. In a stand mixer, beat the eggs until pale yellow, about 1 minute. Add milk and vanilla, then beat until well blended. Add about ⅓ of the egg/milk mixture to flour mixture. Whisk until mixture is free of lumps. Add remaining egg/milk mixture and whisk until smooth.
5. Remove skillet from oven. Carefully whirl the oil around the pan, and immediately transfer the pancake mixture to the skillet.
6. Bake for about 20 minutes. Cut into 4 wedges, transfer wedges to serving plates. Serve immediately with butter and syrup.

4 servings

HIGH-FIBER PANCAKES

This is a nutrient-rich pancake recipe that is good if you need a stick-to-the-ribs breakfast or if you're serving hearty appetites. Because the batter thickens over time, if you don't use all the batter at once, add more milk if necessary to get the initial consistency. Serve with pork or vegetarian sausage, or bacon.

1¼ cups water
½ teaspoon salt
½ cup yellow corn flour
½ cup quick cooking oatmeal
⅛ cup millet
1 egg
2 tablespoons neutral oil
1¼ cups milk or more
¼ cup wheat germ
¼ cup whole wheat flour
⅛ cup flaxseeds, coarsely ground
2 teaspoons baking powder
Butter and syrup

1. In a medium saucepan, bring water and salt to a boil. Slowly stir in corn flour and oatmeal. Stir vigorously. Decrease heat to low and simmer for 3-5 minutes until very thick. Allow mixture to cool.
2. Preheat toaster oven or oven to 350°F. Place millet on a rimmed baking sheet and toast until lightly browned. Watch closely; there's a narrow window between toasted and burned.
3. In a large bowl, combine egg, oil, and milk. Add cornmeal mixture and stir until well combined.
4. In a small bowl, combine wheat germ, whole wheat flour, toasted millet, flaxseeds, and baking powder. Add to the cornmeal/milk mixture and stir until fully combined.
5. In a large skillet, heat oil over moderately high heat. Drop spoonfuls of batter into skillet and cook for 1-2 minutes, or until golden brown on each side. Serve immediately with butter and syrup.

8 servings

SUMMER CORN PANCAKES

When fresh corn is abundant during the summer months, it seems I am always gratefully de-cobbing and making these tasty pancakes. I chop half of the corn kernels because they are a great contrast to the whole corn kernels. Bacon and fried green tomatoes are delicious accompaniments.

2 eggs
2 tablespoons neutral oil
1 cup milk
½ cup yellow corn flour
½ cup unbleached all-purpose flour
1 teaspoon baking powder
½ teaspoon salt
2 cups fresh corn kernels
Butter and syrup

1. In a large bowl, whisk eggs and oil. Add milk and whisk until blended. Add corn flour, all-purpose flour, baking powder, and salt.
2. Roughly chop 1 cup of the corn. Add chopped corn kernels and whole corn kernels to the flour mixture and combine until well blended.
3. In a medium skillet, heat oil over moderately high heat and spoon batter (about ¼ cup per pancake). Lower heat slightly and cook for about 2 minutes on each side. Serve immediately and pass the butter and syrup to your guests.

14 to 16 pancakes

PARSNIP PANCAKES
WITH GINGER PRESERVES

I love how the ginger preserves complement the sweet parsnips in these unusual, albeit popular pancakes. The batter is thick (so thick you might think you're in error), but the parsnips high water content releases when the pancake batter is resting and when the pancakes are cooking. I use James Keiller & Son Dundee Ginger Preserves because they have a pronounced ginger flavor.

1 egg
2 tablespoons milk
½ cup unbleached all-purpose flour
1 teaspoon baking powder
½ teaspoon salt
2 cups peeled and shredded parsnips
Butter and ginger preserves

1. In a medium bowl, combine the egg and the milk. Add flour, baking powder, and salt. Mix until combined. Fold in parsnips. Let batter rest for 15-30 minutes.
2. In a large skillet, heat about 1 tablespoon canola oil over moderate heat. Drop tablespoons of batter into skillet (cook pancakes in batches) and cook until brown on both sides, about 2 minutes per side. Serve immediately with butter and ginger preserves.

About 14 pancakes

BLUEBERRY ALMOND COFFEE CAKE

When these nutrient-rich powerhouses are in season, I can't resist making this moist and aromatic coffee cake.

1 cup unbleached all-purpose flour
½ cup sugar
¾ teaspoon baking powder
½ teaspoon salt
¼ teaspoon baking soda
1 cup fresh blueberries
⅔ cup milk
2 tablespoons neutral oil
1 teaspoon vanilla
¼ teaspoon almond extract
1 egg
¼ cup sliced almonds
1 tablespoon packed brown sugar
¼ teaspoon ground cinnamon
Butter

1. Preheat oven to 350°F.
2. Coat an 8-inch baking pan with cooking spray.
3. In a large bowl, combine flour, sugar, baking powder, salt, and baking soda. Add ⅔ cup of blueberries to the flour mixture and toss until well combined.
4. In a medium bowl, combine milk, oil, vanilla, almond extract, and egg, then whisk until well blended. Add liquid mixture to flour mixture and stir until combined. Transfer batter to prepared pan and top with remaining blueberries.
5. In a small bowl, combine almonds, brown sugar, and cinnamon. Sprinkle over top of blueberries.
6. Bake for 35 minutes or until a toothpick inserted in the center comes out clean. Serve immediately and pass the butter to your guests.

6 servings

ROASTED TOMATOES, LENTILS, AND SPINACH WITH CREAMY SCRAMBLED EGGS

I typically prepare this savory, colorful, and comforting combination on weekends, when we sometimes eat a heartier breakfast, and I also find myself preparing it for midweek lunch and dinner.

ROASTED TOMATOES

4 medium tomatoes, cored and cut in half width-wise
1 teaspoon dried basil
2 cloves garlic, minced
2 tablespoons olive oil
Salt and freshly ground black pepper

LENTILS, SPINACH, AND EGGS

1 teaspoon salt
1 cup red lentils, rinsed
1 bunch fresh spinach
8 eggs
1 tablespoon butter
4 tablespoons cream cheese, softened
Salt and freshly ground black pepper, to taste

1. Preheat oven to 400°F.
2. To prepare the roasted tomatoes, top them with basil, garlic, and olive oil. Season with salt and pepper. Cook the tomatoes for 15-30 minutes, or until they are tender. (Cooking time varies, depending on the ripeness of the tomatoes.)
3. In a large pot, bring 4 cups of water to a boil. Add salt and lentils. Cover, decrease heat, and cook lentils for 30-40 minutes or until tender. Keep warm.
4. In a large pot, steam spinach until just wilted. Keep warm.
5. In a medium bowl, whisk the eggs until well blended.
6. In a large skillet over moderate heat, melt butter. Decrease heat and add eggs. Allow the eggs to cook briefly undisturbed until they begin to set. Stir the eggs using a lifting motion and continue cooking until they are of desired consistency.
7. Remove from heat and place a dollop of cream cheese on top of the eggs. Let them sit for a few seconds. Season with salt and pepper. Stir eggs to distribute cream cheese. Keep the eggs warm while you assemble the rest of the dish.
8. Divide lentils evenly among 4 serving bowls, then top with 2 tomato halves and spinach. Divide scrambled eggs evenly and place next to lentil/tomato/spinach mixture. Serve immediately.

4 servings

POACHED EGGS
OVER BUTTERY SHREDDED WHEAT

As a child, my mother disliked cow's milk. This aversion proved challenging for her mother, especially when it came to what to pour over cold breakfast cereals. So instead of pouring milk over shredded wheat cereal (very popular when my mother was growing up), my grandmother crushed the cereal and sautéed it in butter and seasoned it with salt. It became my mother's all-time favorite breakfast. Breakfasts were many and varied when I was growing up, so when my mother announced she was sautéing shredded wheat, I was thrilled. Fast-forward a few decades when I found myself concocting a recipe in which a perfectly cooked poached egg tops salty, crunchy, buttery shredded wheat cereal. The shredded wheat catches the runny yolk perfectly. (For me, a perfectly cooked poached egg is when the white part is firm and the yolk is runny.) The amount of butter to use in the shredded wheat is a matter of personal preference.

1 tablespoon white or apple cider vinegar
4 eggs
2 tablespoons butter or desired amount
4 servings shredded wheat cereal, crushed
Salt and freshly ground black pepper, to taste

1. Fill a 2-quart pot with 1½ quarts of water. Bring the water to a boil, add vinegar, and decrease heat to medium high. Water should be actively rumbling, but not boiling.
2. Melt butter in a large skillet over moderate heat. Add crushed shredded wheat and sauté until crispy. Season with salt to taste. Set aside.
3. Break egg into a small cup and gently slide egg into rumbling water, working quickly repeat with remaining eggs. Cook eggs for 3-5 minutes or until desired doneness.
4. Divide shredded wheat among 4 rimmed serving plates.
5. Remove eggs with a slotted spoon, drain of any excess water and place egg on top of shredded wheat. Season eggs with salt and pepper. Serve immediately.

4 servings

ZUCCHINI AND EGG CASSEROLE

I love to serve this for brunch when zucchini is at the peak of its harvest. A favorite summer brunch menu: sliced tomatoes, bacon, pork or vegetarian sausage, slices of ciabatta bread, and Peach Crisp for dessert (see page 190).

1 pound zucchini, unpeeled and cut into cubes
½ cup diced onion
6 eggs
½ teaspoon salt
¼ teaspoon black pepper
½ teaspoon dried oregano
½ teaspoon dried thyme
½ teaspoon dry mustard
2 cups shredded Swiss cheese

1. Preheat the oven to 325°F.
2. In a medium pot, steam zucchini and onion until just tender. Transfer zucchini/onion mixture to a bowl and gently mash.
3. In a large bowl, beat eggs with a wire whisk. Add salt, pepper, oregano, thyme, and dry mustard, then whisk until well blended. Add 1½ cups of cheese and zucchini/onion mixture to the egg mixture and stir to combine.
4. Pour mixture into a lightly oiled 1½-quart baking dish. Top with remaining cheese.
5. Bake for 45-50 minutes or until light brown. Serve immediately.

6 servings

sweet bites

Introducing Chocolate Desserts, Pies, Cakes, Crisps, Cobblers, Cookies, Dessert Bars, and More

There is no shortage of choices in this sweet-filled chapter. For convenience (or maybe for whatever kind of sweet you're craving), I've divided the chapter into two parts: one section is purely devoted to chocolate, and the other section has pies, cakes, cobblers, crisps, cookies, and dessert bars. For you chocolate lovers, this is a collection of my very best—don't skip the Chocolate Beet Cake. You will be amazed by how moist the cake is and how well the beets are disguised. Many of the recipes are from my mother's recipe box and evoke childhood memories, especially of birthday celebrations and special occasions. Many of the desserts using fresh summer fruit bring back memories of large family gatherings. What better way to conclude a meal than with something sweet and comforting and a great memory?

CHOCOLATE TRUFFLES

These truffles make a lovely hostess gift. For a pretty presentation, place in decorative bon bon-sized paper party cups.

> *6 ounces sweet German chocolate*
> *4 tablespoons butter*
> *2 tablespoons milk*
> *2 tablespoons liqueur (Grand Marnier, Kahlua, or Cointreau)*
> *Cocoa powder*
> *Confectioners' sugar for dusting (garnish)*

1. In a medium saucepan over moderately low heat, melt chocolate and butter. Add milk and liqueur and stir mixture until well combined. Transfer to a bowl, cover, and refrigerate overnight.
2. Roll about 1 heaping teaspoon of truffle mixture into a ball. Roll each ball into cocoa powder.
3. Lightly dust truffles with confectioners' sugar and serve immediately, or cover and refrigerate until serving time.

About 20 (1-inch) truffles

CHOCOLATE MERINGUE PIE

After one bite, this melt-in-your-mouth pie always gets an ooh-la-la. For cream to properly whip, place mixing bowl and/or beaters in the freezer for about 2 hours prior to preparing whipped cream.

MERINGUE

2 egg whites, at room temperature
½ cup sugar
⅛ teaspoon cream of tartar
½ cup chopped nuts (pecans, walnuts, or almonds)

CHOCOLATE PIE FILLING

6 ounces semisweet chocolate chips
3 tablespoons hot water
½ teaspoon vanilla
1 cup heavy cream

1. Preheat oven to 275°F.
2. Lightly coat a 9-inch pie plate with cooking spray.
3. To prepare the meringue, place egg whites in a large bowl. Beat on medium-high speed with an electric mixer, while gradually adding sugar. Increase speed, add cream of tartar, and beat until whites are glossy and stiff peaks have formed. Transfer meringue to the prepared pie plate. Spread meringue evenly across the bottom and sides of pie plate. Sprinkle nuts over top of meringue and bake for 1 hour.
4. While the meringue is baking, prepare part of the chocolate filling. (The chocolate filling has to cool before it can be added to the whipped cream.) In a medium pan over moderate heat, combine chocolate chips and hot water, then stir until chocolate has melted and mixture is smooth. Stir in vanilla. Set mixture aside.
5. Once the meringue has cooled, prepare the whipped cream. Pour whipping cream into medium bowl and beat on medium speed. When the cream thickens, increase the speed and continue to beat until cream falls in large globs and has soft peaks. Add cooled chocolate mixture to whipped cream and combine until well blended. Spread chocolate filling over cooled meringue shell.
6. Cover and chill pie for 2-3 hours before serving.

6 servings

STOVE-TO-OVEN BROWNIES

Taste-testers say these are the best brownies they've ever eaten.

> *16 tablespoons (2 sticks) butter*
> *4 ounces unsweetened baking chocolate*
> *2 cups sugar*
> *4 eggs*
> *1 cup unbleached all-purpose flour*
> *2 teaspoons vanilla*

1. Preheat oven to 350°F.
2. Generously oil a 13 x 9 x 2-inch baking pan with cooking spray. Dust the coated pan with cocoa powder.
3. In a large pan, melt butter and chocolate over medium-low heat. Remove from heat, add sugar, and stir until sugar is mostly dissolved.
4. In a medium bowl, beat eggs until well blended. Add eggs to chocolate mixture and whisk until eggs are fully incorporated into chocolate mixture. Add flour ½ cup at a time and whisk until flour is incorporated. Stir in vanilla. Transfer batter to prepared pan.
5. Bake for 22 minutes or until toothpick inserted in center comes out clean.
6. Allow the brownies to cool completely before cutting. For precision cuts, refrigerate brownies after they have completely cooled. When the brownies are firm, cut them into squares. For a unique presentation, cut the squares into triangles.

32 (2 x 2-inch) squares

CHOCOLATE PUDDING CAKE

The pudding part in this cake comes from pouring boiling water over the cake batter. During the baking process the water gets partially absorbed by the batter, resulting in a part pudding, part cake-like dessert. Serve this hot from the oven with Sweet Whipped Cream (see page 146) or vanilla, strawberry, or salted caramel ice cream.

1 cup unbleached all-purpose flour
⅔ cup sugar
¼ cup cocoa powder
2 teaspoons baking powder
¼ teaspoon salt
½ cup milk
3 tablespoons neutral oil
1 teaspoon vanilla
1 cup water

1. Preheat oven to 350°F.
2. Generously coat an 8-inch square baking pan with cooking spray.
3. In a large bowl, combine flour, sugar, cocoa powder, baking powder, and salt.
4. In a small bowl, whisk together milk, oil, and vanilla. Add to dry ingredients and mix until fully combined. Transfer batter to prepared baking pan.
5. Bring 1 cup of water to a boil. Pour boiling water evenly over cake. Do not stir.
6. Bake cake for 30 minutes or until cake springs back when lightly touched. Serve immediately.

6 servings

CHOCOLATE BREAD PUDDING

This bread pudding is divine! It's also a great way to utilize any leftover French or Italian bread. Serve with Sweet Whipped Cream (see page 146) into which you've folded a few tablespoons of raspberry jam. It's also good with vanilla ice cream. To keep the milk from burning and/or scorching and sticking to the bottom of the pan, rinse the pan with cold water (don't dry it) right before you add the milk.

3 cups milk
5 cups bite-sized pieces French or Italian bread
6 ounces semisweet chocolate chips
1 egg
⅓ cup sugar
1 teaspoon vanilla
1 teaspoon ground cinnamon
¼ teaspoon salt

1. Preheat oven to 350°F.
2. In a medium pan over moderate heat, heat milk until warm.
3. Coat a 2-quart baking pan with cooking spray. Place bread cubes in prepared pan. Distribute chocolate chips over bread cubes. Add warm milk to the bread/chocolate mixture and let the mixture rest for about 15 minutes.
4. In a medium bowl, combine egg, sugar, vanilla, cinnamon, and salt. Whisk until well blended. Pour egg mixture evenly over bread cubes.
5. Fill a 3-quart baking pan with about ½ inch of water. Carefully set the 2-quart pan into the 3-quart baking pan.
6. Bake uncovered for 45 minutes. Serve hot from the oven.

8 servings

CHOCOLATE BUTTERMILK CAKE

My mother made this cake for as long as I can remember. It's one of those tried and true chocolate desserts that satisfies a chocolate craving. If you don't have buttermilk on hand, add 1 teaspoon of lemon juice or white vinegar to a half-cup of milk.

> *1 cup canola or neutral oil*
> *1 cup water*
> *½ cup buttermilk*
> *4 tablespoons cocoa powder*
> *2 cups sugar*
> *2 cups unbleached all-purpose flour*
> *2 eggs*
> *1 teaspoon baking soda*
> *1 teaspoon vanilla*
> *½ cup confectioners' sugar*
> *1-2 teaspoons water*

1. Preheat oven to 350°F.
2. Generously oil a 13 x 9 x 2-inch baking pan with cooking spray.
3. In a large pan, combine oil, water, buttermilk, cocoa powder, and sugar. Over moderate heat, bring mixture to a boil, stirring occasionally. Remove from heat. Whisk in flour a ½-cup at a time, whisking well after each addition. Whisk in eggs, one at a time. Add baking soda and vanilla, then whisk until fully blended. Transfer batter to prepared baking pan.
4. Bake for 30 minutes or until toothpick inserted in the center comes out clean.
5. In a small bowl, combine confectioners' sugar with water, adding more or less water depending on the desired consistency. Allow cake to cool slightly before drizzling icing over cake.

12 servings

CHOCOLATE PEANUT BUTTER BARS

Hard to go wrong when butter, peanut butter, sugar, and chocolate are combined! Huzzah!

8 tablespoons (1 stick) butter, softened
½ cup chunky natural peanut butter
1 cup sugar
2 eggs
2 teaspoons vanilla
1 cup unbleached all-purpose flour
1 teaspoon baking powder
½ teaspoon salt
12 ounces semisweet chocolate chips

1. Preheat oven to 350°F.
2. Generously oil a 13 x 9 x 2-inch baking pan with cooking spray.
3. In a large bowl, combine butter, peanut butter, and sugar. Whisk until well combined. Add eggs and vanilla, then whisk until smooth. Stir in flour, baking powder, and salt. Combine until well blended. Fold in chocolate chips. Transfer mixture to prepared baking pan.
4. Bake for 25 minutes. Allow bars to cool before cutting into squares.

32 (2 x 2-inch) squares

CREAM-FILLED CHOCOLATE BABY CAKES

These baby cakes are always well-received. If this yield is more than you need, the baked baby cakes freeze beautifully.

> *1 egg*
> *4 ounces light cream cheese, softened*
> *⅓ cup sugar*
> *⅛ teaspoon salt*
> *6 ounces semisweet chocolate chips*
> *1½ cups unbleached all-purpose flour*
> *1 cup sugar*
> *¼ cup cocoa powder*
> *1 teaspoon baking soda*
> *½ teaspoon salt*
> *1 cup water*
> *½ cup neutral oil*
> *2 tablespoons fresh lemon juice*
> *1 teaspoon vanilla*
> *90 2½-inch mini cupcake baking cups*

1. Preheat oven to 350°F.
2. In a medium bowl, beat egg, cream cheese, sugar, and salt until well blended. Fold in the chocolate chips. Set mixture aside.
3. In a large bowl, combine flour, sugar, cocoa, baking soda, and salt.
4. In a medium bowl, whisk water, oil, lemon juice, and vanilla together. Add liquid mixture to flour/cocoa mixture and mix until well combined.
5. Place about 20 mini baking cups on two, parchment-lined, rimmed baking sheets. (Because of the recipe yield, you will have to cook the baby cakes in batches.)
6. Using a small spoon, fill mini baking cups half full with chocolate mixture. Place about a ½ teaspoon or more of the cream filling into the center of the chocolate mixture. (It may seem like you're adding such a small amount of filling, but the cakes need room to rise. Add too much filling and the batter spills out over the cups.)
7. Bake for 15-20 minutes or until a toothpick inserted in the center comes out clean. Transfer to a wire rack to cool.

About 90 baby cakes

CHOCOLATE-COVERED CRACKER COOKIES

It's hard for me to resist anything with butter, sugar, chocolate, and salt. These are finger-licking good—accompany with lots of napkins.

About 54 salted Saltine crackers
8 tablespoons (1 stick) butter
½ cup light brown sugar, packed
6 ounces semi-sweet chocolate chips

1. Preheat oven to 350°F.
2. Line a 17½ x 11½-inch rimmed baking sheet with parchment paper. Line the bottom of the baking sheet with crackers in a single layer.
3. Melt butter in a medium saucepan over moderate heat. Add brown sugar, decrease heat, and allow the mixture to come to a boil, stirring constantly.
4. Evenly pour mixture over crackers (not every part of the crackers will get covered—this will happen while it's baking). Bake for 6 minutes or until the brown sugar is bubbly.
5. Remove baking sheet and turn off the oven. Top the crackers with chocolate chips and return to the oven for 1-2 minutes.
6. Spread chocolate chips evenly across the top of crackers.
7. When cracker cookies have cooled, break into ragged pieces.

About 54 cracker cookies

CHOCOLATE-COVERED OATMEAL CRUNCH SQUARES

Using nuts in this recipe is a matter of personal preference; either way, they are delicious.

8 tablespoons (1 stick) butter
½ cup light corn syrup
½ teaspoon salt
2 teaspoons vanilla
¾ cup packed brown sugar
3 cups quick-cooking oats
12 ounces semi-sweet chocolate chips
½ cup chopped nuts, optional

1. Preheat oven to 350°F.
2. Melt butter in a medium saucepan over moderate heat. Remove from heat and add corn syrup, salt, vanilla, brown sugar, and oats. Mix until thoroughly blended. Transfer the mixture into a 13 x 9 x 2-inch baking pan. Press the mixture into pan and bake for 18 minutes.
3. Top oatmeal mixture with chocolate chips, distributing evenly. Bake for an additional 2 minutes. Using an icing spreader or spatula, spread chocolate evenly over the top of the oatmeal mixture. Sprinkle with nuts, if desired.
4. Allow the squares to cool completely before cutting.

24 squares

CHOCOLATE BEET CAKE WITH CREAM CHEESE ICING

If you're not partial to beets, you may just change your mind after trying one of my most unusual recipes in which I've folded shredded sweet beets into chocolate cake batter. After Nick taste-tested the cake, I asked if he could guess the predominant ingredient. *Applesauce? Buttermilk? Yogurt?* Thrilled with my culinary endeavor, I couldn't wait to share it with my nephew Travis, who warned me before arriving for a weeklong stay that he doesn't eat beets! (My inspiring culinary endeavor was unbeknownst to him.) Travis loved the cake so much he asked for seconds and after devouring his second helping, he asked if he could finish the cake. Guessing the main ingredient has puzzled many a taste-tester, including Travis, who turned into a Chocolate Beet Cake-loving teenager!

CHOCOLATE BEET CAKE
2 medium-size beets, unpeeled and quartered
1 cup unbleached all-purpose flour
⅔ cup sugar
¼ cup unsweetened cocoa powder
1 teaspoon baking soda
⅛ teaspoon salt
¼ cup sour cream
3 tablespoons neutral oil
1 egg
½ teaspoon vanilla
¼ cup reserved beet water

CREAM CHEESE ICING
4 ounces cream cheese, softened
½ cup confectioners' sugar
¼ teaspoon vanilla

1. Fill a medium pot with water and bring to a boil. Add beets and decrease heat slightly (water should be dancing). Cover and cook for 20-30 minutes or until beets are fork-tender. Transfer beets to a medium bowl, reserving ¼ cup of the beet water. When beets are cool enough to handle, pinch the skin away from the beets. Shred the beets after they have cooled completely. You will need 1 cup of shredded beets.
2. Preheat oven to 350°F.
3. Lightly coat an 8-inch round cake pan with cooking spray.
4. To make the cake, in a large bowl, combine flour, sugar, cocoa powder, baking soda, and salt.

5. In a medium bowl, combine sour cream, oil, egg, vanilla, and reserved beet water. Whisk until well blended. Add sour cream mixture to flour mixture and stir until well combined. Fold in shredded beets. Transfer mixture to prepared cake pan.
6. Bake cake for about 22 minutes or until toothpick inserted in the center of cake comes out clean.
7. Allow the cake to cool before transferring to a platter.
8. To make the icing, in a small bowl whisk together cream cheese, confectioners' sugar, and vanilla. Spread icing evenly over the top of the cake.

6 to 8 servings

CHOCOLATE CAKE WITH CRISPY PEANUT BUTTER MARSHMALLOW TOPPING

This nameless recipe was given to me by a friend. The writing was scribbled on a ragged-edged piece of paper riddled with oily splatters. Splatter-filled, hand-me-down recipes are almost always guaranteed to be fabulous! Inheriting this recipe was timely because many family members (this recipe has a big yield) were gathering to celebrate the union between my 80-year-old mother and her friend of a few years. Why not celebrate by eating chocolate? After we bid the duo off on their honeymoon, a bunch of us changed into our jammies, and, with lip-smacking gusto, we ate this crispy, gooey, chocolaty, nutty, gratifyingly sweet dessert. This cake is actually better if made a day in advance.

CHOCOLATE CAKE
8 tablespoons (1 stick) butter, softened
¼ cup neutral oil
1½ cups sugar
3 eggs
1 teaspoon vanilla
1⅓ cups unbleached all-purpose flour
½ teaspoon baking powder
½ teaspoon salt
3 tablespoons cocoa powder

PEANUT BUTTER TOPPING
12 ounces semi-sweet chocolate chips
1 cup chunky natural peanut butter
2 cups Rice Krispies cereal
10.5 ounces miniature marshmallows

1. Preheat oven to 350°F.
2. Generously coat an 11½ x 16½ x 1-inch rimmed baking sheet with cooking spray.
3. To prepare the cake, cream butter with oil in a large bowl. Slowly add sugar. Beat in eggs one at a time. Add vanilla and beat until fluffy.
4. In a medium bowl, combine flour, baking powder, salt, and cocoa. Add flour mixture to wet ingredients and combine well. Transfer cake batter to prepared baking sheet and spread evenly. Bake for 15 minutes.
5. To prepare the peanut butter topping, melt chocolate chips and peanut butter in a medium saucepan over low heat. Stir mixture to combine well. Remove from heat and stir in rice cereal.

6. When the cake has finished baking, sprinkle marshmallows evenly over the cake and return it to the oven for about 2 minutes.

7. Working quickly, spread the melted marshmallows over the cake (don't worry—the marshmallows will not spread perfectly). Spread the peanut butter mixture over the marshmallows. The marshmallows will naturally peek through the peanut butter mixture. Once the cake has cooled, cover and let stand at room temperature before serving.

32 (2 x 3-inch) squares

MOLASSES PIE

I like to serve this delicious pie with Sweet Whipped Cream (see page 146) or vanilla ice cream.

1 (9-inch) unbaked pie shell (see page 132)
1 cup unbleached all-purpose flour
½ cup firmly packed brown sugar
4 tablespoons butter, cut into chunks
1 cup water
1 teaspoon baking soda
1 cup molasses
¼ teaspoon salt

1. Preheat oven to 375°F.
2. In a medium bowl, combine flour, brown sugar, and butter. With the tips of your fingers or with a fork, combine the mixture until it resembles coarse meal.
3. In a medium saucepan, bring water to a boil. Remove from heat and stir in baking soda (mixture will bubble), molasses, and salt. Combine until well blended. Pour mixture into unbaked pie shell. Sprinkle brown sugar mixture evenly over molasses mixture. Place pie plate on a rimmed baking sheet to catch any mixture that might fall on the oven floor.
4. Bake for 10 minutes. Decrease oven temperature to 350°F and bake an additional 25-30 minutes or until light brown. Cool to room temperature before serving.

6 servings

FRESH STRAWBERRY PIE

I recommend preparing this when strawberries are at the peak of their growing season. Dollop the pie wedges with Sweet Whipped Cream (see page 146) or ice cream.

1 (9-inch) baked pie crust (see page 132)
2 tablespoons butter, melted
1 tablespoon sugar
4 cups fresh strawberries, sliced
1 cup water
¼ cup sugar
2 tablespoons cornstarch

1. As soon as the pie crust comes out of the oven, pour the melted butter evenly over the crust. Sprinkle the crust with 1 tablespoon of sugar. Allow pie crust to cool.
2. When the crust has cooled, arrange 2 cups of sliced strawberries in the shell.
3. In a medium saucepan, bring a ½ cup of water to a boil. Add remaining strawberries and sugar. Cook over medium heat for 3-5 minutes.
4. In a small bowl, mix a ½ cup cold water with the cornstarch. Pour into hot strawberry mixture and stir until thick. Pour mixture over strawberries. Allow the pie to cool before covering. Chill for several hours before serving.

6 servings

LEMON MERINGUE PIE

I like to use Eagle brand sweetened condensed milk in this recipe. It's the thickest and most flavorful sweetened condensed milk I tested. It helps to grate the lemon peel before you juice the lemon. To get the most juice from lemons (this applies to all citrus fruits), place the fruit on the counter and roll it back and forth with the palm of your hand. To prevent the meringue from sticking to the pie cutter or knife, coat the utensil with butter before slicing.

1 can (15 ounces) sweetened condensed milk
1 tablespoon grated lemon peel
½ cup fresh lemon juice (2½-3 lemons)
2 egg yolks
¼ teaspoon salt
1 (9-inch) baked pie crust (see page 132)
2 egg whites, at room temperature
3 tablespoons sugar
⅛ teaspoon cream of tartar

1. Preheat oven to 350°F.
2. In a medium bowl, combine sweetened condensed milk, grated lemon peel, lemon juice, egg yolks, and salt. Whisk until ingredients are fully incorporated. Pour mixture into baked pie shell.
3. In a large bowl, beat egg whites on medium high speed and gradually add sugar. Increase speed and add cream of tartar. Beat until egg whites are glossy and stiff peaks have formed. Spoon meringue evenly over pie filling making certain to cover the filling. To create the peaks meringue pies are so known for, use the back of a small spatula or knife and lift the meringue mixture in many places creating small peaks.
4. Bake pie for 10-15 minutes or until meringue is light brown. Allow the pie to cool before serving.

6 servings

Spaghetti Squash Cake
with Ginger Icing

I challenged my culinary creativity and decided to fold one of winter's blandest vegetables into cake batter. I'm known for adding vegetables to pancakes, waffle and cake batters with satisfying results. So I reasoned with myself: if I incorporated this unusual vegetable (once cooked, the flesh of the spaghetti squash separates into strands that resemble spaghetti), would it turn out a great-tasting cake? Taste-testers loved the cake! I use ginger preserves by James Keiller & Son because of the pronounced, authentic flavor.

1 cup cooked and finely chopped spaghetti squash
¼ cup neutral cooking oil
1 egg
2 tablespoons milk
½ teaspoon vanilla
1 cup unbleached all-purpose flour
⅓ cup sugar
⅓ cup packed brown sugar
⅛ teaspoon salt
½ teaspoon ground cinnamon
½ teaspoon powdered ginger
1 teaspoon baking powder
¼ cup ginger preserves
4 ounces light cream cheese, softened

1. Preheat oven to 350°F.
2. Cut the squash in half lengthwise and remove the seeds. Filled a rimmed baking dish with 1-2 inches of water. Place squash halves face down; the halves should be immersed about halfway in the water. Bake for 30-45 minutes or until fork-tender. Remove squash halves from water bath. When they are cool enough to handle, turn them face side up and transfer to a platter. Once cooled, use a fork to rake out the spaghetti-like strands.
3. Generously oil an 8-inch round cake pan with cooking spray.
4. In a medium bowl, combine oil with egg, milk, and vanilla. Add spaghetti squash and stir until well blended.
5. In a large bowl, combine flour, sugar, brown sugar, salt, cinnamon, ginger, and baking powder. Add squash mixture to flour mixture and combine until moistened and well blended. Transfer cake batter to prepared pan.
6. Bake for 20 minutes or until toothpick inserted in the center comes out clean.

7. When cake has cooled transfer to a platter.
8. In a small bowl, combine ginger preserves with cream cheese. Spread icing evenly over cake. Serve immediately.

6 servings

Parsnip Cake
with Cream Cheese Icing

Parsnips generally are as sweet as carrots. When I created this combination, my theory was that if you can successfully add carrots to cake batter, surely parsnips would turn out a similar-tasting cake. Indeed they do; this is a moist and delicious cake.

PARSNIP CAKE
1 cup unbleached all-purpose flour
⅔ cup sugar
1 teaspoon baking powder
⅛ teaspoon salt
¼ cup plain yogurt
3 tablespoons neutral oil
2 teaspoons grated orange rind
½ teaspoon vanilla
1 egg
1 cup peeled and shredded raw parsnips

CREAM CHEESE ICING
4 ounces light cream cheese, softened
½ cup confectioners' sugar
¼ teaspoon vanilla
Slivered orange rind (garnish)

1. Preheat oven to 350°F.
2. Generously oil an 8-inch round cake pan with cooking spray.
3. In a large bowl, combine flour, sugar, baking powder, and salt.
4. In a medium bowl, combine yogurt, oil, orange rind, vanilla, and egg until well blended.
5. Make a well in the center of the dry ingredients, add liquid ingredients, and combine until moistened. The batter will be dense. Fold in parsnips, distributing them evenly. Transfer batter to prepared cake pan.
6. Bake for 20 minutes or until cake is light brown and a toothpick inserted in the center comes out clean.
7. Allow the cake to cool in the pan for about 10 minutes before transferring to a wire rack.
8. To prepare the icing, combine cream cheese, confectioner's sugar, and vanilla in a medium bowl and mix until smooth and creamy.
9. Transfer cake to a rimmed cake platter and spread icing over cake. Garnish with slivered orange rind. Serve immediately.

8 servings

MANGO CAKE WITH CARDAMOM

The idea for this recipe came to me when I had too many ripe mangoes in my fruit basket. The combination of mango and the aromatic cardamom made for a delicious taste-treat dessert.

1 cup bite-sized mango pieces
½ cup raspberry-cranberry juice
2 eggs
⅔ cup sugar
1 teaspoon vanilla
4 tablespoons butter, melted
¼ cup neutral oil
1 cup unbleached all-purpose flour
½ teaspoon ground cardamom
Confectioners' sugar (optional)

1. Preheat oven to 400°F.
2. Generously oil a 10-inch baking dish with cooking spray.
3. Distribute mango evenly in the bottom of the baking dish and pour raspberry-cranberry juice over the mango.
4. In a large bowl, beat eggs and gradually add sugar. Beat until well combined. Add vanilla, butter, and oil, and beat until well combined. Add flour and cardamom, then stir until fully blended. Spoon batter over mango—the mango will show through in some places; cooking will distribute the batter.
5. Bake for 20 minutes or until light brown and bubbly.
6. Allow the cake to cool, then dust with confectioners' sugar if desired.

8 servings

PEACHES AND CREAM CAKE

Don't let peach season slip by without making this delicious cake—pictured on the cover.

CAKE

½ cup butter (1 stick) softened
⅔ cup sugar
1 teaspoon vanilla
2 eggs
1 cup unbleached all-purpose flour
1 teaspoon baking powder
¼ teaspoon salt

FILLING

½ cup (4 ounces) light cream cheese, softened
⅓ cup sugar
¼ cup sour cream
1 egg

TOPPING

4 cups fresh peaches, peeled and chopped
1 cup sour cream
¼ cup light brown sugar, packed

1. Preheat oven to 350°F.
2. In a medium bowl, cream butter with sugar. Add vanilla and eggs and beat until smooth.
3. In a small bowl, combine flour, baking powder, and salt. Add to butter mixture and beat until smooth. Spread cake batter into a lightly oiled 9-inch round baking pan. Set aside.
4. In a medium bowl, beat cream cheese, sugar, sour cream, and egg until well combined. Spoon filling evenly over cake batter. Bake for 30 minutes or until light brown.
5. While the cake is baking, assemble the topping. In a medium bowl, combine the sour cream and brown sugar until well blended.
6. Spread sour cream mixture evenly over the top of the cake. Top with peaches. Serve immediately. Refrigerate any unused portion.

8 servings

AMARETTO CAKE

This is an incredibly moist cake, infused with just the right hint of Amaretto.

3 eggs, separated
1⅔ cup sugar
1 cup unbleached all-purpose flour
½ teaspoon salt
8 tablespoons (1 stick) butter, melted
1 teaspoon vanilla
½ cup milk
1½ cups water
2 tablespoons Amaretto

1. Preheat oven to 375°F.
2. Generously coat a 9-inch tube pan with cooking spray.
3. In a large bowl, beat egg yolks until light. Continue beating while gradually adding ⅔ cup of sugar. Add flour, salt, butter, vanilla, and milk, then beat on low speed until fully incorporated.
4. In a medium bowl, beat egg whites until stiff. Fold egg whites into cake batter. Transfer batter to prepared tube pan. Place pan on a parchment-lined baking sheet to catch any spills that might land on the oven floor.
5. Bake cake for 30 minutes.
6. While cake is baking, combine water and 1 cup of sugar in a medium saucepan. Bring mixture to a slow boil. Cook mixture until thick, stirring frequently, for about 40 minutes. The color will darken slightly as it thickens to the consistency of syrup. Remove from heat, add Amaretto, and stir until combined.
7. Allow cake to cool for about 10 minutes before transferring to a rimmed cake platter.
8. Using chopsticks or a fork, prick several holes in the top of the cake. Spoon syrup over cake. Allow the cake to cool before serving.

10 to 12 servings

PEAR CAKE

I love the depth of flavor that ground cloves add to this simple, aromatic, and rustic-looking dessert. I'm as steadfast as always about using food when it's in season, and pears are no exception. Anjou and Bosc varieties are good cooking pears.

> *2 eggs*
> *⅔ cup sugar*
> *1 teaspoon vanilla*
> *8 tablespoons (1 stick) butter, melted*
> *1 cup unbleached all-purpose flour*
> *2 ripe pears, peeled and sliced or enough to cover the bottom of a 9-inch pie plate*
> *Apple cider (about ¼ cup)*
> *Ground cloves*

1. Preheat oven to 400°F.
2. Generously oil a 9-inch pie plate with cooking spray.
3. In a large bowl, beat the eggs and gradually add the sugar. Add vanilla and butter, and then beat until well combined. Slowly add flour and mix until fully incorporated.
4. Arrange pear slices in the bottom of the pie plate and cover them with apple cider. Generously sprinkle the pears with ground cloves. Spoon dollops of batter over the pears (baking will evenly distribute the batter).
5. Bake for 20 minutes or until light brown and bubbly. Serve immediately.

6 servings

AUTUMN APPLE CRISP

I think fruit crisps are one of the easiest desserts to make, and they're so satisfying. They're a great way to showcase the season's bounty because fruit crisps can be made using just about any fruit or berry. The best apples for crisps are Braeburn, Gala, Golden Delicious, Granny Smith, Jonagold, Pink Lady, Rome, or Winesap. Serve this crisp warm with Sweet Whipped Cream (see page 146) or vanilla ice cream.

4 cups sliced apples (about 4 large)
¼ cup orange juice
¾ cup sugar
¾ cup unbleached all-purpose flour
½ teaspoon ground cinnamon
¼ teaspoon ground nutmeg
8 tablespoons (1 stick) butter, semi-soft and cut into chunks
Sweet Whipped Cream or vanilla ice cream

1. Preheat oven to 375°F.
2. Generously oil a 9-inch pie plate with cooking spray.
3. Arrange apple slices evenly in the pie plate and pour orange juice over apples.
4. In a medium bowl, combine sugar, flour, cinnamon, and nutmeg. Drop chunks of butter into flour mixture and, with your fingers, incorporate the butter with the flour until the mixture is coarse. Sprinkle mixture over apples.
5. Bake for 45 minutes. Serve immediately with Sweet Whipped Cream or vanilla ice cream.

6 servings

PEACH CRISP

I savor the time when peaches come into season. If it didn't seem ridiculous, I'd mark the days off the calendar until peach season begins. I owe my love of this glorious fruit to my grandparents. Our summers were spent vacationing at their rustic cabin in Hagerstown, Maryland. Every August the whole family (nearly 30 of us) gathered for a reunion. We could barely contain our excitement when the day came to eat the hand-churned, homemade peach ice cream their neighbors made. The peaches were picked from their orchard, and the milk came straight from their dairy cows. We savored every spoonful of this aromatic, sweet, creamy chock-full-of-peach ice cream. I've never tasted any ice cream like it since. But peach ice cream wasn't the only luscious treat their peach orchard turned out. Hundreds of mason jars were filled with peaches (for the winter months—what a practical generation!), and just-picked peaches were turned into peach pies, marmalades, jams, cakes, cobblers, and peach crisp. Ah, the glorious gifts of summer's harvest, family, and childhood memories! I like to serve this crisp with Sweet Whipped Cream (see page 146) or vanilla ice cream.

> *4 cups peeled and sliced ripe, juicy peaches*
> *¾ cup unbleached all-purpose flour*
> *¾ cup brown sugar*
> *1 teaspoon ground cinnamon*
> *8 tablespoons (1 stick) butter, cut into chunks*
> *Sweet Whipped Cream or vanilla ice cream*

1. Preheat oven to 350°F.
2. Arrange peaches in a 9 x 9-inch baking dish.
3. In a medium bowl, combine flour, brown sugar, and cinnamon. Drop butter chunks into flour mixture and cut with 2 knives, or use your fingertips, and combine the ingredients until the mixture is somewhat crumbly. Sprinkle mixture over the top of the peaches.
4. Bake for 30 minutes or until bubbly. Serve immediately with Sweet Whipped Cream or vanilla ice cream.

6 servings

CHERRY COBBLER

The cherry season is brief, so don't let it slip by before making this delectable desert. Serve the cobbler hot from the oven with vanilla ice cream or Sweet Whipped Cream (see page 146).

5 cups pitted ripe cherries
½ cup sugar
2 tablespoons cornstarch
¼ cup water
3 tablespoons butter
1 tablespoon grated lemon rind
¼ teaspoon almond extract
1 cup unbleached all-purpose flour
½ cup sugar
1 teaspoon baking powder
½ teaspoon salt
½ cup milk
4 tablespoons butter, softened
1 teaspoon vanilla
1 egg
Sweet Whipped Cream or vanilla ice cream

1. Preheat oven to 350°F.
2. Generously oil an 11 x 7-inch baking dish with cooking spray.
3. In a large saucepan over moderate heat, combine cherries, sugar, cornstarch, and water. Stirring constantly, gently bring mixture to a boil and boil for 1 minute. Remove from heat and add 3 tablespoons of butter, lemon rind, and almond extract. Stir until fully combined. Transfer mixture to prepared baking dish.
4. In a large bowl, combine flour, sugar, baking powder, and salt. Add milk, 4 tablespoons of butter, and vanilla. Beat mixture on medium speed for about 2 minutes. Add egg and beat for an additional 2 minutes.
5. Dollop batter over cherry mixture. (Don't worry if the batter doesn't cover the cherry mixture; it will sort itself out during the baking process.)
6. Bake cobbler for 40-45 minutes or until golden brown.
7. Serve immediately with vanilla ice cream or Sweet Whipped Cream.

6 servings

GINGER MOLASSES COOKIES

I am partial to anything that calls for ginger. Here I've combined powdered and crystallized ginger for a rich ginger flavor.

¾ cup wheat germ toasted
5 tablespoons butter, softened
⅔ cup packed light brown sugar
¼ cup molasses
1 egg
2 tablespoons minced crystallized ginger
1⅓ cups unbleached all-purpose white flour
2 teaspoons baking soda
1½ teaspoons powdered ginger
1 teaspoon ground cinnamon
2 tablespoons sugar

1. Preheat oven to 350°F.
2. Place wheat germ on a rimmed baking sheet and bake until lightly browned. (Watch closely; there is a narrow window between toasted and burned.)
3. In a large bowl, cream butter, adding brown sugar ⅓ cup at a time. Add molasses and egg, then beat until light and fluffy. Stir in crystallized ginger.
4. In a medium bowl, combine flour, wheat germ, baking soda, powdered ginger, and cinnamon. Add to molasses mixture and combine well.
5. Cover dough and freeze for 20 minutes or refrigerate for 1 hour.
6. Generously oil 2 rimmed baking sheets with cooking spray.
7. Lightly oil hands with a neutral oil. Using about 1 tablespoon of dough, shape dough into 30 balls. Place balls in a large rimmed container. Sprinkle sugar over balls and gently shake the container so all the balls catch the sugar evenly.
8. Place balls on prepared baking sheets and bake for 10-12 minutes.
9. Allow the cookies to rest for 1-2 minutes on baking sheet before transferring to wire rack to cool completely.

30 cookies

OLD-FASHIONED SUGAR COOKIES

My mother made these paper-thin, delectable cookies every Christmas. Over the years, she filled hundreds of cookie tins and lovingly gave them as Christmas gifts.

16 tablespoons (2 sticks) butter, softened
1 cup sugar
1 egg
1 tablespoon milk
½ teaspoon vanilla
1½ cups unbleached all-purpose flour
1 teaspoon baking powder
½ teaspoon salt
Additional flour and sugar for rolling dough
1 egg white, lightly beaten
Ground cinnamon and/or naturally colored sugar to decorate the tops of cookies

1. In a large bowl, cream butter while gradually adding sugar. Add egg, milk, and vanilla, and beat until well combined.
2. In a medium bowl, combine flour, baking powder, and salt. Slowly add flour mixture to butter mixture and combine until dough is fully incorporated.
3. Refrigerate for 1½ hours or overnight.
4. Preheat oven to 350°F.
5. Generously cover a work surface with equal amounts of flour and sugar. Divide dough into 6 sections. Roll a section at a time (to get the dough just right, I typically have to roll each section a few times to keep it from sticking to the work surface) until paper-thin or to the thickness you prefer. Cut into shapes and place on a parchment-lined baking sheet. With a pastry brush, brush the tops of each cookie with egg white and sprinkle with desired topping.
6. Bake for 10-12 minutes or until light brown. Transfer to a wire rack to cool. Store in an airtight container.

About 6 dozen very thin cookies

MERINGUE COOKIES

The key to a great meringue is to use superfine (castor) sugar; it dissolves easier in the egg whites than granulated sugar. If you don't have castor sugar on hand, place the measured amount of granulated white sugar in a food processor or use a mortar and pestle and process until very fine. In addition to a meringue the size of a cookie, you can make the meringues bigger and use them as an edible bowl for fresh assorted fruit. To form the bowl, lightly oil the outside of a soup ladle. After you've arranged the desired amount of meringue on the baking sheet, make a well in the center of the meringue to form the bowl. You can add any variety of chopped nuts or candy pieces to the meringue mixture—candied ginger, peppermint candy, chocolate chips, and candied citrus peel are all delicious additions; ¼ to ½ cup is an appropriate measure.

2 egg whites, room temperature
⅛ cup ceam of tartar
½ cup sugar (castor or superfine)
½ teaspoon vanilla

1. Preheat oven to 200°F.
2. Line 2 rimmed baking sheets with parchment paper. To prevent the parchment paper from sliding, place a little oil on the underside of each corner of the paper.
3. In a large bowl, beat egg whites on medium speed until foamy. Add the cream of tartar, increase the speed to high, and continue to beat. When meringue begins to take shape, slowly add the sugar and continue to beat until the meringue is stiff and doesn't feel gritty when you rub a little between your fingers. Add vanilla and beat until fully blended. Fold in addition, if desired. Drop 12 spoonfuls of meringue (or use a pastry bag fitted with a decorative tip) onto parchment-lined baking sheets.
4. Bake meringues for about 1½ hours. After 45 minutes—no sooner, or meringues might crack—switch baking sheets and rotate them to ensure even baking. Bake an additional 45 minutes.
5. Turn off oven and leave meringues in the oven overnight to finish their drying process.

About 2 dozen cookies

PECAN BARS

These dessert bars are rich, decadent, and always well-received!

CRUST
16 tablespoons (2 sticks) butter, softened
⅔ cup sugar
2 cups unbleached all-purpose flour

PECAN TOPPING
11 tablespoons butter
⅛ cup maple syrup
⅛ cup honey
¼ cup molasses
3 tablespoons milk
½ cup brown sugar
3½ cups pecans, chopped

1. Preheat oven to 350°F.
2. Generously oil a 13 x 9 x 2-inch baking pan with cooking spray.
3. To prepare the crust, combine 2 sticks of butter and sugar in a large bowl and beat until well blended. Add the flour ½ cup at a time and mix until the flour incorporates into the butter and sugar. Press the mixture evenly into the baking pan and bake for 20 minutes.
4. To prepare the topping, in a medium saucepan combine 11 tablespoons butter, maple syrup, honey, molasses, milk, and brown sugar. Over moderate heat, stir until the mixture is melted and well combined.
5. When the crust has finished baking, pour the mixture evenly over crust. Top the mixture with pecans, evenly distributing the nuts. Gently press the pecans lightly into the topping. Bake for an additional 25 minutes.
6. When the baking pan has completely cooled, refrigerate for several hours, or overnight, before cutting. For a perfect bar, cut them while they are cold, and allow them to come to room temperature before serving.

24 (2 x 2-inch) bars

LEMON COCONUT BARS

If you're a fan of lemon bars, this rendition—with coconut, cranberries, and walnuts—adds a depth of flavor and texture to this delicious dessert bar. It's easier to grate the lemon rind before you juice the lemon. To get the most juice from a lemon (this applies to all citrus fruits), place the fruit on the counter and roll it back and forth with the palm of your hands before juicing.

CRUST
16 tablespoons (2 sticks) butter, softened
⅔ cup sugar
2 cups unbleached all-purpose white flour

TOPPING
3 eggs
1 cup packed brown sugar
½ teaspoon salt
2 teaspoons grated lemon rind
⅓ cup fresh lemon juice
1½ cups shredded coconut
½ cup dried cranberries
½ cup chopped walnuts

1. Preheat oven to 350°F.
2. Generously oil a 13 x 9 x 2-inch baking pan with cooking spray.
3. In a large bowl, combine the butter and sugar. Add the flour a ½ cup at a time and mix until the flour incorporates into the butter/sugar mixture. Press the dough evenly into the prepared baking pan. Bake for 20 minutes.
4. In a large bowl, beat eggs until bright yellow. Add brown sugar, salt, lemon rind, and lemon juice. Beat mixture until well combined. Pour egg/lemon mixture over crust to cover completely.
5. In a medium bowl, combine coconut, cranberries, and walnuts. Spread coconut mixture evenly over filling. Press mixture lightly into the filling. Bake for 25 minutes. Cool before cutting.

24 (2 x 2-inch) bars

GINGER-FILLED DATES WITH FRESH FRUIT

The Medjool date is commonly referred to as the "king of dates" and for good reason. Their deep amber-brown flesh tastes a bit like rich caramel with hints of honey and cinnamon. The best time to buy fresh dates is when they are in season (the California Medjool date season runs from September through December). You can find them at that time in the produce section of most grocery stores.

8 cups bite-sized pieces of assorted fresh fruit
2 tablespoons Cointreau (optional)
8 pitted dates
8 pieces crystallized ginger (candied)
Sweet Whipped Cream (see page 146)

1. In a large bowl, combine the fruit with the Cointreau and toss to combine. Cover and refrigerate for several hours.
2. Stuff each date with a piece of ginger. Slice each date into thirds.
3. Divide marinated fruit among 8 serving bowls and top each bowl of fruit with 3 pieces of the stuffed date. Top each bowl with a dollop of Sweet Whipped Cream. Serve immediately.

8 servings

PEACH GALETTE

If you're not familiar with the word "galette," it is used in French cuisine to designate various types of flat, round, or free-form crusty cakes that are often made of pastry and topped with fruit or vegetables. I love to prepare this peach galette when peaches are in season. It's good with a dollop of frozen raspberry yogurt, gelato, or sorbet.

GALETTE
1 cup unbleached all-purpose flour
1 tablespoon sugar
¼ teaspoon salt
⅓ cup neutral oil
2 tablespoons cold water

FILLING
2 tablespoons all-purpose flour
5 tablespoons sugar
½ cup ground almonds
4 medium peaches (about 2 pounds), peeled and thinly sliced
2 tablespoons butter, cut into small pieces

1. To prepare the galette, in a large bowl combine flour, sugar, and salt. Drizzle oil over flour mixture and toss with a fork. Add water and knead a few times. Gather the dough into a ball, cover, and refrigerate for 30 minutes or overnight.
2. Preheat oven to 375°F.
3. Line a rimmed baking pan with parchment paper.
4. Lightly flour a work surface and roll the dough into a 14-inch diameter round. If dough begins to resist, let it sit for about 5 minutes. Carefully transfer the dough to the parchment-lined baking pan.
5. To prepare the filling, in a small bowl combine flour, 4 tablespoons of sugar, and the almonds. Sprinkle the almond mixture evenly over the dough.
6. Arrange peach slices in the center of the dough, leaving a 1- to 2-inch border. Fold the edges of the dough over the peaches (the center will remain exposed) and sprinkle with the remaining sugar. Top the galette with butter pieces.
7. Bake for 45 minutes or until peaches are bubbly and crust is golden brown. Serve immediately.

6 servings

dog treats

INTRODUCING ALL-NATURAL DOG TREATS

Nick and I could have never imagined the joy that Artichoke, a Norwich terrier, would bring to our lives as we drove him home in a torrential rainstorm many years ago. He was already 2½ years old when we picked him up on that wet, chilly November morning in 1997. Crated and in an unfamiliar car with unfamiliar people, he was justifiably nervous. I reached back, petted him, looked into his trusting eyes, and told him how certain I was that the three of us were destined to be together.

And destined to be together we were. Though Nick and I had enjoyed an exceptionally wonderful life together, it took less than one day for Artichoke to become the center of our world. For the next twelve years, we lived and breathed Artichoke. Three walks around the block practically every single day brought out many new two-legged friends as well as four-legged ones. We hosted dog parties (the treats in this section were always on the menu), and all of our friends wanted to buy Norwich terriers. The neighborhood children set up an "Artichoke Watch!"

We re-entered him into the show ring (he had been a champion before he came into our lives), enrolled him in obedience school, and made him the recurring star of our annual Christmas card (sometimes he even agreed to dress in full holiday regalia). We took him to Westminster shows, as well as regional shows where we met Norwich lovers of all kinds. He was even Mr. October in the 2000 Norwich/Norfolk Terrier calendar. Better known as the stud-muffin, Artie had girlfriends at every bank and grocery store in our neighborhood.

He was an all-around champion and an endless source of enjoyment for us. Artie died the day after Christmas in 2008. All you dog lovers know how hard it is to lose a dog, but I take comfort in all the things we did for Artichoke. I especially have wonderful memories of making him the dog treats that appear in this chapter. He loved them!

About ten months after Artichoke died, we received an e-mail about a Norwich terrier in Richmond, Virginia, whose owner died suddenly. After a telephone interview with the owner's daughter, we got into the car and headed to Richmond. We met Copper Penny (named for her copper coloring, but called "Penny" for short) and fell in love. The three of us got into the car with Penny right in between us and headed home. We immediately renamed her Caramel. Caramel fills our days with happiness, love, and tons of kisses!

DOG TREATS

MILK AND MOLASSES DOG TREATS

1 cup whole wheat flour
1 cup unbleached all-purpose flour
½ cup rye flour
¼ cup corn flour
1 teaspoon salt
½ cup raw sunflower seeds, chopped
2 tablespoons olive oil
¼ cup molasses
2 eggs
¼ cup milk

1. In a large bowl, combine whole wheat flour, all-purpose flour, rye flour, corn flour, salt, and sunflower seeds.
2. In a medium bowl, combine olive oil, molasses, eggs, and milk. Mix until well blended. Add mixture to dry ingredients.
3. Place dough on a lightly floured work surface and knead (the dough is dense) for 2-3 minutes to fully incorporate the dough. Cover and let the dough rest for 30 minutes.
4. Preheat oven to 325°F.
5. Line 2 baking sheets with parchment paper.
6. Roll dough out to approximately ¼-inch thickness and cut into 1½-inch squares or use a biscuit cutter. Transfer to the prepared baking sheets and bake for 25-30 minutes. Turn the oven off, but keep the biscuits in the oven for an additional 30 minutes. Transfer them to a wire rack and allow them to cool completely before transferring to an airtight container.

4 to 5 dozen treats

Peanut Butter Dog Treats

1½ cups whole wheat flour
½ cup wheat germ
1 tablespoon brown sugar
1¼ cups smooth natural peanut butter
¾ cup milk

1. Preheat oven to 400°F.
2. Line 2 rimmed baking sheets with parchment paper.
3. In a medium bowl, combine whole wheat flour, wheat germ, and brown sugar.
4. In a large bowl, beat peanut butter and milk on a low speed. Gradually add flour mixture and mix until well combined.
5. Transfer dough to a work surface and knead for about a minute—dough will be very stiff.
6. Roll out to ¼-inch thickness and, using a biscuit cutter, cut into 1½-inch rounds. Transfer to the prepared baking sheets and bake for 12-15 minutes. Cool on a wire rack before transferring to an airtight container.

About 6 dozen treats

WHOLE WHEAT DOG TREATS

2½ cups whole wheat flour
¼ cup raw wheat germ
½ cup dry milk powder
½ teaspoon salt
6 tablespoons neutral oil
1 egg
1 tablespoon molasses
½ cup cold water

1. Preheat oven to 375°F.
2. Line 2 baking sheets with parchment paper.
3. In a large bowl, combine whole-wheat flour, wheat germ, dry milk powder, and salt.
4. In a small bowl, combine oil, egg, molasses, and water. Mix until well blended. Add mixture to dry ingredients. Knead dough a few times or until ingredients are fully incorporated.
5. Roll dough out to ¼ inch thickness, and cut into 2-inch squares or use a biscuit cutter. Place on prepared baking sheets. Bake for about 20 minutes. Cool them on a wire rack before transferring to an airtight container.

About 5 dozen treats

BARLEY DOG TREATS

1 cup unbleached all-purpose flour
1 cup whole wheat flour
½ cup barley flour
½ cup dry milk powder
½ cup raw wheat germ
1 tablespoon brown sugar
1 egg
2 tablespoons neutral oil
½ - ¾ cup water

1. Preheat oven to 325°F.
2. In a large bowl, combine all-purpose flour, whole wheat flour, barley flour, dry milk powder, wheat germ, and brown sugar.
3. Stir in egg, oil, and a ½ cup of water. Combine until well incorporated. If dough seems dry, add an additional ¼ cup of water.
4. Transfer dough to a floured work surface and knead for a few minutes. Roll dough to about ½-inch thickness and cut into 1½-inch square biscuits.
5. Place on a parchment-lined baking sheet. Bake biscuits for 30 minutes. Cool them on a wire rack before transferring to an airtight container.

4 to 5 dozen treats

PRODUCT AND FOOD GUIDE

BAKING CUPS
I use baking cups from If You Care because they use premium-quality, unbleached, grease-proof paper. No chlorine is used in the production, so no chlorine is cast into our lakes, rivers, and streams. Free of Quilon, which contains heavy metals, like chromium, that can be toxic when incinerated, If You Care uses silicone, derived from a natural element. For more about its vast environmentally friendly line of products and store locator, go to **www.ifyoucare.com**.

BAKING POWDER
There are some baking powders on the market that contain aluminum. Read the ingredient list on the baking powder you may already have in your kitchen or before making a new purchase. There are a few brands of aluminum-free baking powder available; most major supermarkets and health food stores carry them.

CHICKEN BROTH
When I was growing up, my mother made the most memorable soups and stews using her homemade chicken broth. I fully endorse homemade broth, but if time is of the essence, Imagine Organic Free Range Chicken Broth is a full-bodied brand that comes closest to the flavor of the broth my mother prepared (I tested nearly every organic broth on the market). Imagine can be found in most grocery stores nationwide, or find it by going to **www.imaginefoods.com**.

CHOCOLATE BLOOM
When chocolate is stored in overly warm or humid conditions, the cocoa butter rises to the surface. This creates a grayish coating called "bloom," and although it looks like some interior cabinet ghost may have dusted the chocolate, it is perfectly fine and the "bloom" doesn't affect flavor. Once baked, the grayish coating disappears.

CORN – DE-COBBING
Buy corn at the height of its growing season when it's most plentiful and delicious. I cook large quantities, de-cob, and then freeze for year-round use. Easily remove the long, clingy strands of silk from ears of corn by brushing off silk with a firm-bristled toothbrush while holding the corn under cool running water. After you've cooked the corn and allowed it to cool, place a rimmed baking sheet in the sink. Cut the tip of the cob to create a flat end. Starting from the top, with a sharp paring knife slice the corn as close to the cob as possible (you can usually cut about 4 rows at a time), removing corn until you've reached the bottom of the cob. Do this until you've finished removing all the kernels from the cob. With the dull side of the paring knife, use the same technique to extract any extra juice and the heart of the kernel from the cob.

CRUMBS – CRACKER VERSUS BREAD
Cracker crumbs come from whole crackers and are crushed or processed in the food processor into a fine crumb. Bread crumbs are the result of bread that has gone stale or hardened and then crushed or processed in the food processor into crumbs that are not as fine as cracker crumbs. I recommend using homemade cracker and bread crumbs instead of the store-bought versions; they have a much better texture and flavor, and are ultra-easy to prepare.

EGGS
Eggs keep from three to five weeks when refrigerated. It's best to keep them in the pulp container because it insulates the eggs and helps maintain moisture. For environmental reasons, try refraining from buying eggs in foam or plastic containers—foam and plastic never leave Planet Earth. Whether brown or white, it's all the same inside. Ever wonder what the white rope-like strands in the egg white are called or their purpose? It's not the beginnings (contrary to popular belief) of an embryo. It called the chalazae (kuh-LAY-zee) and holds the yolk in place. The more prominent the chalazae, the fresher the egg!

EGGS – BEATING WHITES
Eggs are easier to separate when they're cold, but the egg whites will beat to a higher volume when allowed to come to room temperature. So separate just out of the refrigerator and let stand until they come to room temperature, about 15 minutes. The condition and type of bowl in which you beat the egg whites really makes a difference. Bowls should be glass, ceramic, or metal, and should be dry and free of any residual oil, precisely what prevents whites from whipping.

MANGOES – VARIETIES
There are many varieties of mangoes, but the Champagne mango is my favorite and the preferred mango for mango lovers. It's slightly smaller, golden yellow, and has a smoother, creamier texture than some of the other varieties commonly found in grocery stores or food markets. Champagne mangoes are left on the trees until they reach perfect maturity for picking. If you can't get your hands on Champagne mangoes, there are oodles of other varieties available. Mangoes are best eaten when they are ripe; a ripe mango will yield to slight pressure. If you can't find a ripe one, place in a paper bag at room temperature until the flesh yields. The ripening process can take several days.

MANGO – FLESH REMOVAL
To get the flesh of the mango, slice lengthwise on both sides as close to the pit as possible. Criss-cross cut the pulpy side of each piece and then turn inside out by holding each half with both hands and pushing in on the skin side. (Think about turning an orange or lemon wedge inside out.) Once you've got the fruit exposed, cut the mango from the skin. You can get some additional fruit from the top and bottom of the remaining section, which contains the pit.

ONIONS

It's best to store onions in a dry place. If you refrigerate onions, moisture causes them to spoil. To prevent tears when cutting onions, place onions in the refrigerator for several hours prior to cutting. The cold suppresses the onion's release of sulfuric acid compounds, which cause tears when cutting.

PIE CRUST

I seldom use store-bought pie shells, but when Wholly Wholesome was introducing its organic pie shells, the company sent me samples. I was impressed with them—very homemade-tasting. For more information and to find a store locator, go to **www.whollywholesome.com**. If I were ever in a pinch and couldn't prepare a homemade crust, Wholly Wholesome would be my first choice.

PINEAPPLE

Most people think preparing a fresh pineapple is difficult. To the contrary, it's really very simple and well worth the effort. Sometimes pineapples hit the grocery stores not yet ripe, so plan accordingly as the ripening process will take a few days. To detect a ripe pineapple, pull one the central leaves from the top of the pineapple. If it comes out easily, it's ripe. Another method is to smell the bottom; if it has an intense sweet flowery aroma, chances are the pineapple is ripe. To prepare a pineapple, lay it on its side, slice off the top and bottom. Stand the pineapple up and begin cutting off the skin making vertical slices from top to bottom. Once the skin is removed, remove the hard circles. Cut pineapple into slices about 1-inch thick, remove hard, fibrous core, and cut into desired-sized pieces.

POTATOES

Certain varieties of potatoes are better for mashing, baking, frying, and roasting. The starchy varieties turn out fluffy potatoes like mashed, whipped, or twice-baked potatoes. These hold their shape well and are good to use in salads, soups, and stews. Here's a general guide to follow:

For baking and frying use russet (aka Idaho) and Yukon Gold.
For roasting use less starchy potatoes like red, Yukon Gold, heirloom, and red, or white fingerlings.
For mashed or whipped use Yukon Gold, red, or russet.
For salads use white, red, or purple and/or fingerlings.

TOMATOES

I recommend using Muir Glen Organic Tomatoes for their authentic tomato flavor. Since the company's founding, it has been committed to helping farmers choose to grow tomatoes organically. All of Muir Glen's tomatoes are field-grown and vine-ripened under certified organic practices—no synthetic pesticides, no chemical fertilizers. To find a store location near you or to order online, go to **www.muirglen.com**.

VEGETABLE BOUILLON CUBES

If you're a vegan, a vegetarian, or just someone who loves vegetable bouillon straight, or as a base for soups, sauces, etc., I've found a cube that I love to recommend: Rapunzel Vegan Vegetable Bouillon with sea salt. Rapunzel offers a line of three full-bodied vegan bouillons, and while I prefer the regular with sea salt, it also makes one with herbs and another with no salt added. Rapunzel products are available at most health-oriented grocery stores nationwide.

SEASONAL COOKING—
THE FARMERS MARKET DU JOUR

Throughout my childhood, following food seasons was our way of life—we never ate tomatoes in December, zucchini in February, or peaches in April. Why is it so important to buy food in season from your home state or the nearby surrounding region? Purchasing in season supports local communities and farmers. In addition, food purchased from local farmers typically is harvested within hours of purchase; therefore because it hasn't traveled long distances, and it hasn't lost its valuable nutritional content or stressed the environment. It's less expensive especially if it comes from your home garden, a farm stand, a pick-your-own farm, or a local farmer. Aren't these enough reasons to buy fresh produce in and around your home state? To get started, all you need as your guide is your state's harvest chart. Harvest charts can be obtained online by state.

Until the middle of the 20th century, fruits and vegetables were largely harvested from home gardens, nearby farmers, or community gardens. There weren't vast choices—simply what the season presented. For generations born since the 1970s, this may seem hard to imagine, given today's supermarkets in which an endless variety of produce is offered, no matter what the season, circumstances, or consequences. For example, today's consumer can buy asparagus year-round. When not in season locally, asparagus comes from China, Peru and Mexico. But not so long ago, when asparagus came into season it was a delicacy, consumed and appreciated in abundance. When the asparagus season finished its growing cycle, it wasn't seen again until the following spring when the green shoots broke through the soil and it was enjoyed once more.

Following the natural rhythm of a growing season's food cycle changed in the mid-1960s when California began shipping the extensive variety of their produce all over the country. General stores that supplied dry goods were expanding and supplying California-grown fruits and vegetables. Soon local farm stands were slowly going by the wayside. Americans began eating fruits and vegetables that were in season in California, but not necessarily in many other parts of the country.

No other type of fresh produce product exemplifies the exploitation of seasonal eating more than strawberries. In the beginning of the summer and for a short period of time, in my home state of Maryland, this vibrant plant promises aromatic, sweet, juicy, fire engine red berries. One of my fondest childhood memories is of summer days when I tagged along with my dad to work in the city. I recall the A-rabs, men with pony-drawn carts whose deep voices bellowed, "Marrrrr-ynn berries, come git ya Marrrrr-lynn berries, Marrrrrr-lynn berries, git um now," echoing though the streets. Dad and I would stock up, buying several pints of strawberries—one or two for the ride home and the rest for breakfast and my mother's delicious strawberry pie.

Many foods are indigenous to certain states and won't grow in certain climates. A good example is artichokes, a vegetable I love. Nearly 100 percent of fresh artichokes come from California, where they are the official state vegetable. None are grown in Maryland. The height of their duel seasons occurs near the beginning of April and then again in October. During those times, my husband, Nick, and I eat them on a regular basis. As a Marylander, I can justify artichokes from California—as well as coconuts, oranges and lemons from Florida, grapefruit from Texas, and mangoes, limes and bananas from Mexico. Eating foods indigenous only to certain geographic regions and climates is justified when you can't get them otherwise.

I look forward to the harvest seasons of many different kinds of produce, and when a particular fruit or vegetable is not in season, I use what I've traditionally preserved or purchase commercially preserved or frozen food. Consuming these kinds of foods, harvested in season is not merely acceptable; it's preferable to "fresh" produce that was grown thousands of miles away and traveled thousands of miles before landing in the produce aisle.

The best way to follow the seasons is to use a harvest chart for your area as a guide. Food seasons differ from state to state and region to region. Your local farmers will be the most accurate because they provide what they grow. While your harvest chart acts as a guide, keep in mind that every year and every season differs slightly; some produce items might come earlier than expected or later than usual because of different weather occurrences or rising or falling temperatures.

To find out what's in season, you can access an online harvest chart by state. If you shop in grocery stores year-round, remember to check your harvest guide before shopping so you buy the produce that's currently in season. Just because it's in stock doesn't mean it's in season.

Every choice we make is a step closer to maintaining the natural balance that nature intends for us and Planet Earth. Following food seasons allows you to realize all the interesting seasonal culinary discoveries and delicious possibilities.

ONLINE ECO-CULINARY RESOURCES

I've compiled a list of online eco-culinary-related resource sites that share my sincere passion for becoming aware of and responsible for the condition of Planet Earth. These sites demonstrate their work and efforts to reach this goal. Every ounce of our combined efforts toward this end makes these sites worth the time and energy we can collectively devote to incorporating their information into our daily lives and spreading the word about their respective missions and philosophy.

I've carried this theme from my earlier writings. If you have a copy of my cookbook Tasting the Seasons, you're probably familiar with a section in the cookbook titled "Eco-terms, Eco-tips, and Eco-techniques" that provides additional Web sites and other resources on fair trade, organic, sustainable, and other eco-related topics.

Below is a an alphabetical list of online sites—including those referenced this cookbook, that anyone interested in seasonal, healthy cooking will appreciate.

ECO WEBSITE RESOURCES

Earth 911: The vision and mission of Earth 911 is to create a community that helps consumers find their own shade of green and match their values to their purchasing behavior, adopt environmentally sound practices, and drive environmental changes that can have an impact. The site delivers a mix of targeted content, eco-conscious products, and environmentally sound actions so people can live a happier, healthier, sustainable lifestyle that protects our wonderful planet. **www.earth911.com**

Natural Resources Defense Council: The NRDC's mission is to safeguard the earth, its people, plants, and animals, and the natural systems on which all life depends. **www.nrdc.org**

Organic Consumers Association: This is a public interest organization campaigning for health, justice, and sustainability with a focus on the crucial issues of food safety, industrial agriculture, genetic engineering, children's health, corporate accountability, fair trade, environmental sustainability, and other important key topics. **www.organicconsumers.org**

Recycle Bank: Recycle Bank's goal is to inspire smarter choices for a more sustainable future. The site emphasizes that individual actions, such as increasing recycling and learning about greener ways to buy, consume, or dispose of products, can have a big impact on our planet. **www.recyclebank.com**

Seafood Watch: Seafood Watch recommends which seafood to buy and which to avoid. It helps consumers select items that are fished or farmed in ways that have less impact on the environment. **www.seafoodwatch.org**

EDUCATIONAL FOOD SITES

Edible Communities: This site's aim is to transform the way consumers shop, cook, eat, and relate to local food. Through its print publications (look for an Edible Communities publication in your state), Web sites, and events, Edible Communities strives to connect consumers with local growers, retailers, chefs, and food artisans, enabling those relationships to grow and thrive in a mutually beneficial, healthful, and economically viable way. **www.ediblecommunities.com**

Food Tank: Food Tank focuses on building a global community for safe, healthy, nourished eaters. The site spotlights environmentally, socially, and economically sustainable ways of alleviating hunger, obesity, and poverty, and to create networks of people, organizations, and content to push for food system change. **www.foodtank.com**

James Beard Foundation: The foundation's mission is to celebrate, nurture, and honor America's diverse culinary heritage through programs that educate and inspire. Food is economics, politics, entertainment, culture, fashion, family, passion, and nourishment. The James Beard Foundation is at the center of America's culinary community, dedicated to exploring the way food enriches our lives. **www.jamesbeard.org**

Mother Earth News: This provides wide-ranging, expert editorial coverage of organic foods, country living, green transportation, renewable energy, natural health, and green building, Mother Earth News is lively, insightful, and on the cutting edge. It also is the definitive read for the growing number of Americans who choose wisely and live well. **www.motherearthnews.com**

Sustainable Table: Sustainable Table celebrates local sustainable food, educates consumers about the benefits of sustainable agriculture, and works to build community through food. **www. sustainabletable.org**

The World's Healthiest Foods: The George Mateljan Foundation for the World's Healthiest Foods was established by the founder of Health Valley Foods to discover, develop, and share scientifically proven information about the benefits of healthy eating, and to provide the personalized support people need to make healthy eating enjoyable, easy, quick, and affordable. **www.whfoods.com**

WORLDWIDE CULINARY ORGANIZATIONS

Outstanding in the Field: Outstanding in the Field was founded in 1999 when Jim Denevan came up with the idea of setting a table on a farm and inviting the public to an open-air feast in celebration of the farmer and the gifts of the land. He devised a traveling feast with a central vision of farmers, chefs, cheese makers, ranchers, foragers, and wine makers in delicious communion with the people they sustain. Since its founding, Outstanding in the Field has organized more than 600 events and more than 60,000 people have come to farms, ranches, sea coves, vineyards, and rooftops to understand, learn about, and celebrate the farmer. **www.outstandinginthefield. com**

Slow Food: Slow Foods envisions a better, cleaner, and fairer world that begins with what we put on our plates and makes the point that our daily choices determine the future of our environment, economy, and society. Good, clean, and fair food should be accessible to all and should celebrate the diverse cultures, traditions, and nationalities that comprise the United States. **www.slowfoodusa.org**

WEBSITES REFERENCED IN *THIS BOOK COOKS*

Leftover Containers: Page, xix. Vintage glass food storage containers with glass tops can be purchased from the Container Store. **www.containerstore.com**

Old-Fashioned Challenge: Compost, page, xvi and xvii. Organic Gardening offers a simple way to get started. **www.organicgardening.com**

Plastic Wrap: Page, xix. Instead of using plastic wrap to cover food, linen dish covers are fitted with elastic around the edges. They stay snugly in place to protect bowls of prepped vegetables, casseroles, etc., and will help you purge disposable materials from your kitchen. Each wrap is made from sustainably farmed 100 percent unbleached Russian linen, lined with American grown (and woven) organic cotton. Made in California. **www.quitokeeto.com**

The Re-Purposing Challenge: Regrowing food, page, xv and xvi. Mother Nature News has directions for regrowing food that are simple and brief with accompanying photographs. **www. mnn.com**

INDEX

A

almond (s):
  blueberry almond coffee cake, 158
  celery amandine, 93

Amaretto cake, 187

apple (s):
  apple barbecue sauce, 141
  autumn apple crisp, 189

apricots:
  teriyaki walnuts with amaretto cream and
    apricots, 31

artichoke (s):
  spaghetti with shrimp and artichokes in
    spicy tomato sauce, 56
  spicy Mediterranean couscous with beans
    and vegetables, 60
  the classic cheese and artichoke dip, 12
  zesty artichoke dip, 7

aspic:
  bloody Mary aspic, 111
  tomato raspberry aspic, 112

autumn apple crisp, 189

avocado (es):
  Greek shrimp salad with lemon dressing,
    101
  guacamole, 3
  refried bean dip, 4
  red cabbage salad with mango, avocado,
    feta, and cashews, 108

B

bacon:
  bacon-stuffed potatoes, 96
  bacon-wrapped breadsticks, 22
  creamy cheddar and potato soup with
    bacon, 44

bacon, cont:
  filet of beef with bacon, blue cheese, and
    sun-dried tomato stuffing, 71

baked spinach with cheese, 89

baking cups:
  product and food guide, 205

baking powder:
  product and food guide, 205

basil:
  basil-drenched fusilli with shrimp, peas,
    and tomatoes, 104
  summertime tomato pie, 66
  sun-dried tomato and pesto cheese torte,
    29

beans:
  chili rellenos casserole, 73
  easy creamy bean dip, 8
  Halloween soup, 35
  refried bean dip, 4
  roasted tomatoes, lentils, and spinach with
    creamy scrambled eggs, 159
  simple chili, 75
  spicy Mediterranean couscous with beans
    and vegetables, 60
  vegetarian black bean enchiladas, 58

beef:
  apricot meatballs, 17
  beef and broccoli soup, 39
  beef pot roast, 74
  braised beef brisket, 68
  creamy chipped beef and cheese dip, 13
  filet of beef with bacon, blue cheese, and
    sun-dried tomato stuffing, 71
  Italian wedding soup, 36
  marinated beef tenderloin, 69
  simple chili,75
  tamale pie, 67

dips, cont:
  creamy Mediterranean dip, 9
  creamy shrimp dip, 6
  easy creamy bean dip, 8
  refried bean dip, 4
  savory Swiss and onion dip, 10
  smoked fish and horseradish dip, 11
  the classic cheese and artichoke dip, 12
  zesty artichoke dip, 7

dried fruit:
  teriyaki walnuts with amaretto cream and
    apricots, 31
  chicken and leek soup with wild rice and
    prunes, 45
  ginger-filled dates with fresh fruit, 197
  see also specific fruits

dressings, see salad dressings

dumplings:
  chicken and dumpling soup, 41

E

Edam:
  baked spinach with cheese, 89

egg dishes:
  poached eggs over buttery shredded wheat,
    160
  roasted tomatoes, lentils, and spinach with
    creamy scrambled eggs, 159
  zucchini and egg casserole, 161
  see also product and food guide, 206

eggplant:
  caponata, 143

enchiladas:
  vegetarian black bean enchiladas, 58

F

feta:
  baked spinach with cheese, 89

feta, cont:
  fusilli with sun-dried tomatoes, pine nuts,
    and feta, 63
  green bean salad with gingered walnuts,
    cranberries, and feta, 109
  red cabbage salad with mango, avocado,
    feta, and cashews, 108
  spaghetti with shrimp and artichokes in
    spicy tomato sauce, 56
  spinach, rice, and feta casserole, 57
  zesty artichoke dip, 7

filet:
  filet of beef with bacon, blue cheese, and
    sun-dried tomato stuffing, 71

fish:
  curried tuna salad with cranberries and
    cashews, 103
  smoked fish and horseradish dip, 11

flank steak:
  broiled Oriental flank steak, 72

flaxseed:
  flaxseed bread, 119
  wheat bread with millet and flax, 127

Fontina:
  polenta with roasted peppers, tomatoes,
    and creamy Fontina, 62

fresh fruit:
  ginger-filled dates with fresh fruit, 197

fresh strawberry pie, 180

fritters:
  cheddar and cauliflower fritters, 24

G

ginger:
  ginger-filled dates with fresh fruit, 197
  ginger-glazed chicken, 76
  ginger molasses cookies, 192
  green bean salad with gingered walnuts,
    cranberries, and feta, 109

tomato (es), cont:
spaghetti with shrimp and artichokes in
spicy tomato sauce, 56
summer tomato and shrimp salad, 102
summertime tomato pie, 66
sun-dried tomato and pesto cheese torte,
29
tomato raspberry aspic, 112
see also product and food guide, 207

truffles:
chocolate truffles, 165

tuna:
curried tuna salad with cranberries and
cashews, 103

V

vegetables:
seasoned vegetable medley with melted
cheese, 85
see also specific vegetables

vegetable bouillon cubes:
product and food guide, 208

W

wafers:
saga creamy brie and pecan wafers, 27

walnuts:
teriyaki walnuts with amaretto cream and
apricots, 31
green bean salad with gingered walnuts,
cranberries, and feta, 109
maple cranberry sauce with walnuts, 142
red cabbage salad with cranberries, walnuts,
and Roquefort, 107
zucchini salad with warm walnut dressing,
113

wheat bread with millet and flax, 127

wild rice:
chicken and leek soup with wild rice and
prunes, 45
Halloween soup, 35

wontons, wonton wrappers:
crispy fried creamy vegetable wontons, 28
wonton chips, 16

Z

zesty coleslaw with peanuts, 105

zucchini:
creamy chicken and zucchini casserole with
herb stuffing, 77
layers of summer's harvest, 88
seasoned vegetable medley with melted
cheese, 85
vegetable bisque, 47
zucchini and egg casserole, 161
zucchini salad with warm walnut dressing,
113

ABOUT THE AUTHOR

After her mother passed away, Kerry wanted to honor her life and culinary legacy in This Book Cooks. The book blends her mother's culinary and entertaining style and traditions with Kerry's lifelong love and knowledge of all things food.

As the owner and operator of a successful catering business in her hometown of Baltimore, Maryland, Kerry has been a widely read food columnist, culinary consultant, sought-after food judge, and recipe developer for more than three decades. Kerry regularly appears at farmers markets doing demonstrations titled "Seasons with the Farmers and Kerry." She teams with a variety of farmers, food vendors and artisans to showcase their farm-fresh bounty in recipes from her cookbooks.

She lives in Baltimore's historic Tuscany-Canterbury neighborhood with her husband, Nick, and their Norwich terrier, Caramel. She won the national Benjamin Franklin award for her earlier cookbook, *Tasting the Seasons.* She is at work on a cookbook about tomatoes.

SPEAKING ENGAGEMENTS AND COOKING DEMONSTRATIONS

Kerry Dunnington provides talks and cooking demonstrations to organic food markets, educational institutions, farmers markets', special group meetings, in private homes, and on television.

In her presentations, she teaches people how to make their way in the kitchen and turn food into appealing, delicious meals. She offers useful, innovative cooking, entertaining, and time-saving strategies for everyday eating as well as formal and informal entertaining. She demonstrates how to host with style, grace, confidence, and ease.

Throughout each talk and demonstration, Kerry peppers the conversation with educational and informative information about why menu design is important for variety and health and the nutritional and environmental benefits of following food seasons. She offers a variety of tips for how to put together diverse, colorful, and nutritional meals that will please the entire family.

In the spring of 2015, Kerry also began traveling to farmers' markets to bring the farming community together and showcase their food. This project, "Seasons with the Farmers and Kerry," highlights vendors and farmers' fruits, vegetables, herbs, spices, dairy, nuts, seafood, chicken, meats, and condiments. She turns all of these into dishes made from the recipes in her cookbook and presents the many ways seasonal products can be used.

Whether you're tying apron strings on for the first time or looking to improve your cooking skills—or you simply want fresh ideas—here is a sampling of what you can learn from Kerry's presentations and demonstrations.

- How to use your time efficiently and turn out great-tasting meals.
- How to design seasonal, complimenting, colorful holiday menus.
- How to implement successful techniques for making bread.
- How to build simple, colorful, nutritious, balanced meals.
- How to build confidence in the kitchen.

And so much more.

To learn more or to book Kerry for speaking engagements or design your own cooking class or demonstration, contact:
Sarah Gallagher at Artichoke Publishers
speaker@artichokepublishers.com

Coming Soon:
"Tomatoes by the Season"

In *Tomatoes by the Season*, culinary artist Kerry Dunnington writes about one of her favorite foods—tomatoes. This love affair began at a very young age when her mother, aunts, and grandmothers would sit around the kitchen table and talk about the tomato season and all the delicious possibilities it offered.

The book begins with a fresh and motivating round of Kerry's well-known food challenges. Pat Sullivan, president of Slow Food Baltimore, writes an engaging, funny, surprising, and informative piece on the history of tomatoes. Pat also contributes a comprehensive piece on preserving the tomato harvest, teaching readers how to dry, freeze, can, and roast tomatoes. The book has sections devoted to tomato varieties, tips on canning tomatoes, and growing the best tomatoes from tomato enthusiast Laura Genello, farm manager for the Johns Hopkins Center for a Livable Future.

The cookbook has seven exciting tomato-based chapters with recipes using heirloom and summer tomatoes, sun-dried tomatoes, fire-roasted tomatoes, preserved tomatoes, tomato sauces, and oven-roasted tomatoes. In addition to Kerry's inspiring recipes, chefs from all over the United States and Canada were queried for their best tomato recipes, and their contributions include not only excellent recipes but engaging stories drawn from their culinary careers.

Kerry's recipes have useful, inspiring introductory material further enhanced by stories drawn from her rich and varied life experiences in cooking, dining, entertaining, and serving. For tomato lovers, this cookbook offers a rich collection of classic, prized, easy-to-follow recipes for appetizers, soups, salads, entrees, and side dishes.

In this volume, Kerry continues to stress the importance of implementing family food traditions and acknowledging that our culinary choices have a major impact on the environment. Her contributions in her work and cookbooks continue to influence future generations about the importance of shopping the harvest, appreciating nature's bounty, and sharing in the goodness and nourishment that the best home cooking provides.